# The Gift... of Believing

By Rob McGuffey

Published by The Gift... Publishing Company, Inc.

Cover Art by SelfPubBookCover.com

Print Design/Layout by Lorie DeWorken, MINDtheMARGINS, LLC

First Edition

ISBN: 978-0-9991841-0-3

Printed in the United States of America.

# Table of Contents

# Introduction

*Dear new friend...*

We pray for it, we sometimes need to feel for it. We hope for it, sometimes we live in it.

In our humility it flourishes...with our pride it can quickly evaporate.

As we mature, we begin to cherish it, to hopefully even begin to understand it.

*What is this gift?*
*Where does it come from?*
*How can we sustain it?*

I think we all know... to a certain degree. If we take a little more time in our lives to learn how to nourish it, it will have great, lasting effects and wonderful and far reaching consequences in our own lives, and in the lives of others.

Everything good and whole and lasting comes from pure and worthy belief. There is so much in this age of ours that works solely via electronic, scientific or mechanical resources. We seem to have mastered the art of "If I can see it, I'll believe it."

There have been and are great minds that have helped to foster a grand and wonderful, yet sometimes dangerous and frightening world. And new tools, now at hand for so many, who can afford them, bring first-rate power and abilities for many of us to function on this earth quite comfortably. We can access instant news and entertainment from around the globe in clear, concise video in the palm of our hand in any one of a thousand different devices that can excite our minds and stoke our imaginations. Yet... I believe we are in the palm of Another's hand, and He delights in us... much more than we know...

We've all been given the gift... of believing, in varying degrees throughout our lives. If we take a moment to ponder this truth, we might find within ourselves, a key that opens the door to other gifts we have been given to more deeply fulfill our own life's work of art.

Some days when I awaken, very early in my sixth decade, I recognize and embrace the wonder of it all, and other days, I sometimes need to try to stretch my belief enough to comfortably rise from my bed. It was in one of the days that I awoke filled with wonder though, that the spark I had been on the lookout for, the theme to my telling of some of the stories of my life, was made clear to me.

Interestingly enough, it emerged from a spirit of humility, which I suppose for many of us, is sometimes as illusive a virtue as can be, and other times is about our only recourse.

Our stories are our stories, and when I came to terms with the fact that I would publish my own, it was a bit of a revelation. But was there a theme woven throughout my life, and if so, would this theme be reflected in the title of my first and possibly subsequent books? Kind of an important question I thought. With that, I had, months before, prayed for inspiration regarding this very query. After so many years of life, I knew that I should let that prayer go like a feather in the wind, trusting that someday, in Another's time and place, I would have my answer.

And a mere six months or so later…it came.

In the very first moments of my waking on February 2$^{nd}$, 2013, in a gentle and spontaneous instant, I understood how my stories would be presented. Before I even opened my eyes for the day, I sensed my book's title and with that, it's theme, and even words for a new introduction. It was accompanied with that feeling of joy that comes with a long awaited inspiration, an epiphany moment really. And so, after reveling in a bit of elation, I resolved to pen whatever I would write that morning, and after rising and taking some time to settle in, I sat down to begin.

And as quickly as the title, theme and new first paragraph had flowed through my mind, just minutes before, the first lines seemed to vanish from my plate in an instant. My delight in their discovery turned to a slight sense of panic. It all just seemed to disappear so soon after it had unfolded within me. The immediate joy I had experienced in this revelation had shortly thereafter, led to a feeling of pride that the wonderful words that poured out of my mind were all mine.

Well, they were mine, but not all mine. By virtue of the gift of our births, I believe we are co-creators. This coupling is ingrained in our human and spiritual natures, yet so often we forget, or maybe even have not yet discovered that every one of us has a co-pilot.

Of course our first, flesh and blood ones are our mothers. And my own played an inspiring one this unforgettable morning in my life. It was the second Anniversary of my Dad's death, and I would touch base with Mom to make sure she was ok. I thought it best to keep the good news of my title at bay, knowing it could wait just a few days as I felt a quiet determination to just be present with her.

And I was surprised to hear that mom's morning was going rather well, and so I ask her why.

And she answers in such a joyful manner, "Your sister and I were at the Mass this morning that was offered up for Dad, and it was beautiful. I felt peace and somehow that he was looking down on us. But then I was a bit distracted. I couldn't keep my eyes off the red banner hoisted high above on the right side of the altar. And I kept wondering if there was some hidden meaning why it wouldn't leave my gaze. I kept trying to concentrate on the prayers being offered, but to no avail. Was it because your sister Tina had been telling me that it was my belief in her that was helping her through some tough times? I thought maybe, but then that just didn't feel quite right."

I ask my Mom "What did the banner say?" She answers, "Just one word...BELIEVE."

I decide to ease my mom's conscience and let her know what I *believe* to be the reason for her experience, that same morning's long-awaited arrival of the title of my first book...*The Gift...of Believing.*

The stories you will read were written in life, many of them, a long time ago, and some just recently. I've known for some time that although told on many occasions to a number of people, these accounts would one day be written for a much greater consumption. I believe and agree that to everything there is a season, and a time to every purpose under heaven.[1] I'm thankful that it appears that now is the point in time for me to share them in print. Thank you for being a part of this new chapter in my life.

And although I've known that I would become a writer, it has really only been a year or so that the specific seeds of this book and the ones that may follow have been germinating in my mind and heart. You see, I've had some experiences in this life that I know to be valuable to more than just myself, my family and those that I teach. I know this by the reaction of folks to whom I impart these encounters with. I have been given the gift of personally sharing in the look of joy, surprise and spontaneous belief on faces of young and old alike when the climax of one of my true tales is expressed. It blesses my own belief and I emerge from each engagement with confidence that the person I have just spoken with has been enriched not just by whatever gifts I may possess, but by the One in whom I believe.

---

1. Ecclesiastes 3:1

Sharing some very cool things that have happened to me, in the time that I feel is right, with the person that I believe I should be sharing with has often led to very nice experience for both myself and the other. I can tell by their reactions, and I know it is right. I now share with you.

I'll begin with the same story that I've told in my first religious instruction class for 8th grade Confirmation students every one of the last twenty-three years.

It seems like the right place to start.

# Chapter One

# The Throat...

---

*Before we truly believe in something,*
*it helps a great deal to begin to encounter something.*
*And before we encounter something,*
*a prerequisite may be... to listen.*

---

Have you ever been part of a miracle? If you have, what a wonderful thing you've experienced. I'm sure having been so engaged changed your perspective, if not your whole outlook on life. If you don't think that you have been part of the miraculous, you may be right...or perhaps you really have played an integral role in an amazing and heaven-touched story and were never aware.

I was almost twenty-four years old during the latter part of 1977. The most important thing in my life was my faith; yet my level of faith, or understanding of God and His ways, during my first twenty-two years might probably have scored only about a 4 on a scale of 1 to 10. But quite suddenly, personal revelation of God's love for me shortly after graduation from college changed my life, my own perspective, really everything for me in the blink of an eye. By God's providence, I've remained relatively faithful to Him ever since. How could I not? The Love that was gifted to me was the Love that anyone, anywhere would have hoped for, but never in a million years could dream of. It was...perfect, a perception of grace that to my heart, to my entire being was undeniably divine. My life changed in a mere moment. Not only did I recognize that to the very core of my being, but within a relatively short period of time, my family did as well, as the Love that I felt on the inside was also manifesting itself on the outside. Those in my life at that time witnessed a remarkable shift and change in behavior, attitude and presence. I am so glad that God came into my life, and yet that... in and of itself...is a story for another day...

And so, fast forward two amazing years; I put my college degree on hold as I began to seek to discover the meaning of so great a gift to someone such as myself.

I begin to naturally gravitate toward the Church, yet my initial experiences did not originate there. God had become real to me and so I felt compelled to share this Love that I was experiencing with those who possibly knew Him too, as well as with anyone else who I might meet. My Mom always said I wore my heart on my sleeve, and now I felt I had a bit more to share.

And of course as those within most religions know, and as I was finding out, ministry is such an integral part of the expression of God's Love. So I listened to what I believed to be God's leadings and began to do something I had always wanted to do but never did much of...and that was to sing.

And my singing led to my family's establishment of a Christian Coffee House in the basement of the Catholic school that I attended as a child. Something new, something far different for all of us emerged; a small and growing community of relatively young believers learning to share what they were feeling as God's love, through song and service.

We soon outgrew the facility and moved to the larger basement of the chapel where I had received my First Holy Communion many years before. We all felt God's love moving among us in ways we had never imagined. It was there that we meet Roseann.

Roseann is a nineteen-year-old freshman at Adelphi University in Garden City, NY in the early spring of this year. Young, pretty and smart she seems to exude excitement in anticipation of all that life has to offer. On her way out with some friends this one Friday night, she agrees to join them for a few hours at our "Sign of the Dove" Coffee House. Dressed for disco and admittedly not knowing what a coffee house might be, she amiably, though cautiously, joins them.

The lights are low, with lit candles on each round table seating six or eight, mostly young adults with a smattering of some older. Two young men in their early 20s are already on the stage, sitting off its edge, guitars in hand and welcoming the crowd just settling in and taking their seats.

Their attire, jeans and T-shirts, mirrors the casual atmosphere of the venue. They begin to sing. Cool melodies that are a combination of soft rock and folk joined with harmonies that are unusually well timed and synched. Roseann is interested, but a little confused. They're singing about…Jesus? She sits perplexed, but open and somewhat interested, though within ten minutes, she is looking at her watch wondering when she and her friends can get their night started out dancing.

She stays through the first set of music, and at the break, perhaps beginning to settle in herself, saunters to the coffee bar. A middle-aged couple is tending it and they readily greet her with warm smiles. Roseann makes a statement and asks a question of them. With a slightly sarcastic tone she comes out with, "Those boys are singing about Jesus….Did they go to college?" The woman smiles and answers lovingly, but with some pride, "Well, yes!" her chin rising and head tilting almost imperceptibly. "And those boys are my sons."

Slightly embarrassed, Rosanne answers that it's perfectly fine that they're singing about Jesus and then quietly slips away back to her friends, wondering what she got herself into. She stays for the second set, and then not quite sure what she has experienced, comes back the next week, and then the next.

Her interest begins to turn into acceptance. She is finding a new relationship with her God and begins to share it with her old friends and to form friendships with her new. Then, quite naturally, she joins in our ministry and finds another place that she can call home. Roseann came from a loving family; however she might have described them as traditional Catholics, not much like the expressive ones she had just come to know and truly feel a part of. Her life is changing in ways she hadn't expected as she becomes an integral member of our community, displaying a wit and charm that makes everyone want to be her friend, including me.

So much was going on in my own young life in those early years. I'm two years into a rediscovery of myself, my God, my faith and my Church. I very much like what I'm finding.

I hadn't really attended Mass during most of my High School years and never during college. Although I had a Catholic grade school upbringing, the meaning of those things that I learned in religion class never seemed to sink in very deeply. Sports and friends had always taken precedence in my life. Now, with a number of meaningful, spiritual experiences under my belt, and some profound and solid teaching, I'm beginning to feel that I have a somewhat deeper grasp of who God is and what He might possibly be calling me to do with my life. But it was most always a walk in faith, life sometimes seeming to fly and other times, simply put, a struggle.

And it seemed, my faith was always tried and tested, as is the case with all of us I think, who begin to discover and develop the gifts we have been given.

It surely was the same for Roseann, who experienced one of the greatest tests of her life, not long after her own deep and sudden conversion.

After picking a bouquet of daisies and yellow and white marigolds to bring to an elderly neighbor in the hospital, she and her friend Susan are in a horrific car accident.

Their attempt to turn off of Hempstead Turnpike in East Meadow is slowed somewhat due to the relatively heavy traffic just prior to rush hour on this bright, sunny beautiful afternoon of September 14, 1978. The few minutes they are waiting feels much longer as

Susan slowly begins her turn into a parking lot after the drivers of the two cars in the two oncoming lanes stop and give their nods.

As Susan goes hand over hand, Roseann recalled her mom's caution to always be aware that the passenger of a car has as much responsibility to watch traffic as the driver. So she cranes her neck to try to view the last lane which is actually reserved for buses. She neither sees nor hears anyone or anything approaching.

Unfortunately, the oncoming car, speeding at almost 80 MPH in the 40 MPH bus lane is not at all visible until it is too late. Roseann's life flashes before her eyes, but another of her mom's teachings comes in that same instant as well. Roseann's mother, Marie had actually prepared her and her siblings for such an emergency, teaching all of them to alert the driver as soon as they are aware of an impending accident and to always protect your head. So in that same second Roseann screams, "Susan, we're gonna get hit!" as she raises her arms, grasping the back of her head with her hands and shifts her body left, away from the sure-to-be impact, as much as she is able.

The sound of this crash rivals its fury. It sounds and feels like an explosion. The great force thrusts Roseann, Susan and their small car hurtling through the air. The only thing that stops them from completely flipping over is unfortunately another car. It was being driven by a mother with her stunned passengers, her four-year-old daughter and the little girl's grandmother. These three are miraculously unhurt.

The passenger door on Roseann's side is about destroyed, although still joined to the car in a cruel fashion. The smell of the mangled cars, burned tires and antifreeze fills the small cabin. The bucket seat of the green Ford Pinto she had rested comfortably in just a few moments before is crumpled as are a number of Roseann's bones.

Immediate shock ensues for them both, and looking at Roseann's apparent injuries Susan shrieks, "Roseann, are you ok???" Although not having a clue she slowly answers "Yes, I think so...", as the pain from what she has just experienced has not exactly set in just seconds after the crash. Both obviously are in a total state of shock.

Within just a few minutes, sirens blare and brave men of Nassau County's finest are on the scene, as well as one who would become Roseann's earthly angel, a 26-year-old Nassau County Medical Center Registered Nurse. She had been on her way to work and just a half mile shy of her destination. The blonde and blue-eyed beauty speaks to her in a loud, clear and confident tone. "I am a registered nurse. You have been in a bad car accident. What is your name?" Roseann answers clearly. The nurse responds, "I promise I will not leave you Roseann. I will be by your side until the police and fire department can free you and get you in the ambulance. The hospital is less than a mile away, and I will come to see you soon after you arrive."

Roseann places her trust in her angel of mercy as well as in her God, whose presence she feels even as the deep pain begins to set in, in so many places in her young and now, more than ever before, fragile body.

Susan is unhurt, as is the 20-year-old male driver of the offending vehicle which had broken Roseann's body in so many places that it would take days of intensive observation to number. Yet even in these horrific moments, Roseann wants to make sure that Susan is ok, and even inquires as to the health of the young driver who crushed their car, but not her spirit. Roseann has never lost her tender heart.

Because the rush hour traffic impeded their response, East Meadow Fire Department personnel and vehicles could not arrive as quickly as the nimble squad cars of the local police. The initial attempts to free Roseann from the vehicle are stalled and fraught with a tension beyond what might occur in many car accidents.

As is widely known, *Time Magazine* had listed the Ford Pinto at the time as one of the 50 worst inventions in modern history, as it had a tendency to explode when involved in rear end collisions. With that knowledge, the police worked feverishly to find a way to extract young Roseann as fast as they could. An early attempt to move her through the driver's side door, against the advice of her angel nurse led to screams of pain as Roseann couldn't tell if it was her neck, her back, her ribs or her hips. But what she did know for sure was that the attempt to free her makes her aware that she has almost totally lost her breath. She breathes out as loud as she is able voicing, "PUT ME DOWN…I CAN'T BREATHE!" Her helpers immediately realize this is an ill-advised decision and as gently as possible let her back down into the crumpled seat. At this moment, they all take their own breaths, as the officers begin to search each other's brains and hearts for a Plan B. Roseann begins to sense the helplessness of those that have come to rescue her.

She also is aware that she is in an agony she never could have imagined when she was picking flowers less than an hour before, as every breath she takes from here on out accompanies a torment she has never known. But even in these moments, all in attendance are amazed at her continued ability to converse keenly and intelligently, even at times with her quintessential brand of humor, as dark as it needed to be this day.

As the police are concerned that she might lose consciousness at any moment, they know they need her to stay awake, so every few minutes they ask Roseann, "What is your name?" After what felt like the hundredth time, Roseann blares, "Would someone please get a pen and paper and write my name down? I've answered that question at least six times already!!!!" It helps to break the tense mood for all, but she is not even close to being out of the woods on this unforeseen and scary early evening.

After several failed attempts to pry open the door, the police order all to leave the immediate scene, even the nurse, as they need to foam spray the entire car for fear of explosion. Roseann's nurse assures her that she will be only twenty feet away and within her sight at all times. Although not understanding the reason for the foam, Roseann trusts her angel and hangs in there.

Workers from the surrounding stores gather at a safe distance to view the catastrophe. Two stock boys from Modell's Supermarket run to see the mangled wreckage. They return to the store and recount the aftermath to another stock boy, Steven. They tell him that if anyone had been sitting in the passenger seat, they likely didn't make it. Steven, seventeen, is Roseann's younger brother, and he has no idea of the peril his sister is in, but he says a prayer for anyone who may have been hurt.

The Fire Department arrives on the scene and one of the first things one member does is ask Roseann her name. Ugghhh!!!!!

Two of the largest and strongest men begin yanking on the door to no avail. "We gotta get her out!" the biggest one barks. Her nurse, now much closer, calls to her that she now sees the ambulance, "Hang in there, Roseann, they're coming!" she asserts.

Several minutes elapse, Roseann is drained, the pain beyond intense and now she starts to feel warm. It's maybe sixty degrees outside, but the temperature is sweltering, her perspiration pouring down her forehead. She doesn't know what is happening. She uses her remaining strength to painfully inch up a little higher out of her slouched position to see what is going on, and she sees a fireman blow torching the hinge of the passenger door, just inches from her. She yells sarcastically, and as loudly as her weakening condition will allow, "You can't think of something else? I'm going to broil in here!!!"

After a several more minutes of what became near scorching heat, the door is off its hinge and her escape is underway, some fifty minutes after the ominous impact.

Roseann is gently picked up and tenderly placed and secured onto the gurney, and despite this new intense torture, she is relieved to be freed as she looks up at the sun and the unclouded blue sky above, a very much welcomed sight. She thanks her God.

For fear of her critical state, the ambulance driver jumps a curb to get past the traffic during the half mile race, and Roseann feels every bump and turn as somewhat of a new and unwelcomed experience. There is no rest for the weary on this day for Roseann.

As fate would have it, and as Roseann would not know, all three of her siblings have her in prayer so shortly after her accident. Yet neither of her brothers initially knew that the person they were praying for...was Roseann. As she and her gurney are wheeled into the emergency room, her older brother John, twenty-one, is actually sitting in the hospital cafeteria looking out the window. He sees his sister entering, although he doesn't realize it is her. John is an NCMC Orderly and about to go on his nightly shift. As soon as Susan is able, she calls Roseann's home and Roseann's younger sister Lucille, just twelve years old, answers the phone. Susan asks her to put her mom on the phone, and Lucille knows that something is terribly wrong as Susan cannot hold back her sobs. Lucille turns to God and prays for her big sister, not knowing nearly how much her prayers are needed. Very early on in her evaluation as a multiple trauma patient John is allowed to be by her side, even though her own parents need to wait an agonizing seven hours to see their eldest daughter and her fight for her life.

At one point in her evaluation, the doctors lament aloud to her hearing, wishing that they had prior healthy X-rays to compare with these new but slightly puzzling pictures. Roseann motions for a pad and pen. She writes that her healthy X-rays are on file in this very hospital since she had been a candy striper volunteer there as a senior at East Meadow High School. These help greatly in her diagnosis.

Her doctors ultimately determine that Roseann has broken at least eight (8) ribs, two (2) vertebrae, two (2) bones in her pelvis, the Superior and Inferior Rami. She has a collapsed lung, bruised kidney and internal bleeding. The source of the bleeding is yet undiscovered, as she remains in critical condition in the Surgical Intensive Care Unit. She is intubated and put on a respirator as her stunned family holds vigil for her life.

Her parents are finally let in to see her around midnight and her dad, Russell, quietly asks the doctors to order that the entire staff make sure that Roseann is not told of the seriousness of her condition for fear it would hamper her fight to recover. Russell and Marie are told that it is possible that Roseann might not make it through the early hours of the morning.

With what seemed like her last ounce of strength, and with the same pen and pad she had earlier summoned, she writes to her mom and her dad three things:

1. Please call a priest.
2. Please call the McGuffey's. The weekly prayer meeting is on Thursday night, and we need them all to pray.
3. Call Adelphi University and ask them to send back this semester's tuition check. I'm going to be here for a while.

Marie calls the next morning and my mother assures her of two things. We would go to visit as soon as possible, and she would call Mother Angelica and her sisters for prayer. My parents were lay missionaries for Mother at the time, well before the birth of EWTN

Eternal Word Television Network, which would become the largest Catholic Television Network worldwide.

Our T.V. Studio is under roof - Hope to have the boys down one day

Photo of the miraculous image of the Holy Infant Jesus of Good Health, venerated at Morelia, Mexico and propigated by the Franciscan Sisters, Chapel of Prayer, 1526 N. Fresno St., Fresno, Ca. 93703 (Mailing ad. P.O. Box 6118)

Dec. 30th

Dear Drake and Rita, -

Thank you for the record.

We pray Jesus to grant you many graces during this holy Christmas Season and all through the Year 1979.

Jesus and Mary bless you!

Prayerfully,

Mother M. Angelica

Abbess

MCA 231005

The record is beautiful -

Mom calls the Birmingham, Alabama home of Mother and her Sisters and reaches Sister Mary Raphael. Sister asks mom to let Marie know that Roseann's name would sit on the altar of the chapel in Our Lady of the Angels Monastery and that Mother and all of the sisters would pray for her healing and recovery. My mom would often note that, "When Mother and the Sisters pray, things happen."

My brother Dan and I go straight to the hospital, Dan bringing with us, a bottle of holy oil that he had received as a gift that very week. Ordinarily only family is allowed in to see critical patients under such grave circumstances, but the head nurse was told we were from Roseann's church. She is a believing Christian and we are ushered right in.

Seeing her in such a state is surely a shock. Roseann is on a respirator and there are more tubes in her than we could have imagined, but we are immediately impressed with the fierceness of her spirit. It just penetrates our own. Without her being able to speak a word, she conveys through her eyes that she is in control, and that she has God's help.

After communicating our concern to her, we gently ask if she would like us to pray with her and she nods ever so slightly in agreement. We lay hands on her head, pray for the Lord's compassionate intercession as we anoint her with the holy oil. We then trust that our friend and young, brave soul will recover, not having a complete understanding of the harrowing night she has just endured, but nonetheless knowing that she will be in for the long haul.

And so Dan and I visited with her throughout her stay, bringing in our guitars and singing God's praises right in her room amidst hospital carts, IVs and more. We were kind of surprised on more than one occasion, when we noticed out of the corners of our eyes, several nurses huddled outside her door, listening to our every note.

Roseann had been told that she might be in the hospital for up to six months. After a little over one month, she was home. Her long-term therapy had begun with her goal to be able to walk unaided. It was no surprise to any of us as we heard that Roseann continued to make amazing progress.

My brothers and sisters and I continue our ministry, experiencing a leading, day to day, unlike those of the natural stirrings of our early youth. We are continually learning to listen to a voice other than our own; we are maturing and also learning to mature in a spiritual sense. These are for us days where believing is truly a gift, and the wonder of life abounds. Believing in the One we are coming to know is as natural as breathing the air that we breathe, and as joyful an experience as anyone can imagine. We are a part of a fellowship of young believers who are all experiencing and growing in our faith in our own, special and unique ways.

And there is genuine excitement in the air in 1978. Although the Bee Gees and Grease top the music charts, we are singing something quite different as we trend away from the popular culture that had so captivated our teenaged years. We are learning about... prayer. We are learning, really for the first time, about effective prayer. We are learning that there is much more to spiritual life than the formal prayers we had grown up with, the rote recitation of Our Fathers, Hail Marys and Glory Bes, no matter how profound these prayers truly are.

One Tuesday night, I am sitting in my usual section of the lower church of Our Lady of Mercy parish in Hicksville, NY, listening to an anointed soul, Father James Brassil.

Father Jim is known for his close and intimate relationship with God, his Irish brogue, his short stature and his cherry red face. OK, I'll say it. Folks would say he reminded them of a leprechaun.

He is speaking to us in the enchanted way that only Father Brassil can, teaching us about listening prayer. Every soul in every pew is eager to soak up the wisdom that we had come to believe was not solely his.

Father Jim explains that there are really two parts of true prayer, just as there are two parts of human interaction. As we must speak and listen to others, we must also speak… and listen to God. He reminds us that all too often, while praying to God, we just speak. We ask, we may even implore God's great goodness and help, but we often neglect to really listen for His answers, and our relationship with Him is thus left severely one-sided.

So he cajoles us. "The next time you go to pray to God, don't ask Him for anything… just listen to Him."

I take his words to heart, and resolve to do just that the next morning.

My parents were very supportive of their children's journeys in faith. In fact, I was still living in their home during that time in my life. As I was out late the night before with some in the community after the prayer meeting, I awaken a bit late, around 10am. After breakfast, I retreat to my room to take up this new prayer experiment. I am going to just… listen.

I had also been recently taught that praying in your most comfortable position is a very good thing. Nearly abandoning the kneeling that I had been taught growing up in the '60s, my prayer now took on the most comfortable position I could imagine…lying, flat on my back.

I make the sign of the cross, close my eyes and just begin to listen. And for a few minutes I hear… absolutely nothing. But I quietly persist and continue to try to listen.

After several moments, something happens, something that had never happened to me before. I see something.

My eyes are completely closed. I am completely awake. And I see… in my mind's eye, something very unusual.

I view, as if I am watching a black and white movie, what appears to be an image of the inside of someone's throat, with a flap of skin, opening and closing.

I double check my state of consciousness. Am I awake? Yes, I am. Am I dreaming? No, I am awake. Is this my imagination? No, it's a totally new type of experience for me. Not a dream, not my imagination, certainly not a memory. I have a deep sense that I know that God is speaking to me… about what, I surely have no idea, but I am convinced of the authenticity of the experience and that it has to hold some significance.

It is so strange and it came so completely out of the blue.

Shortly after this "listening prayer encounter" I descend the stairs of our two-story Levitt home in the small hamlet of Carle Place, NY and meet my mother, Rita in our living room. I am so excited to tell her of my experience, and so I do. And when I do, her reaction is not what I had anticipated. Since that day, there have been so many times in my life when my mother has confirmed some of my personal prayer experiences and has provided helpful discernment to me, but this time her reaction is not at all what I had expected. In my attempt to discern her somewhat inquisitive look, I tell her, "Mom, it's not gross! I think God is trying to tell me something!" Her facial expression only deepens as if to further question where I am going with this.

I am not fazed, although I certainly have no idea what this message could mean. So I just trust that I will someday find out. And then, just a few moments later the phone rings. I'm really surprised and happy to hear its Roseann.

It had been only six weeks since she came home from the hospital and she would finally be sprung from her house for a few hours. She asks what I will be doing that night and I tell her I am going to visit with my High School friend Billy who is about to be married. I'll be singing at his wedding in a few weeks as I had written a song especially for him and his bride-to-be Janet. I ask Roseann to join me and she is very excited to do so.

It is a really nice reunion. I pick her up at seven p.m. and we head over to see the soon-to-be newlyweds. I recall vividly the sweet love that Billy and Janet shared with each other that seemed to just envelop everyone around them. They were certainly young lovers, the same age as me, and now beginning to share their new life together.

After we arrive and settle in, I take out my guitar and begin to sing. They appear to truly take pleasure in the gentle, love song I had written for them. They ask me to continue so I play my guitar for a while and sing a few more songs. Roseann sings a little with me on a John Denver tune. We then have coffee and cake and they excitedly tell us all about their wedding plans and about their choice of their honeymoon spot. After an hour, we wish Billy and Janet well, and get on our way.

We are not one step out the door and Roseann says, "Let's go somewhere!" Since she hadn't been out for such a long time she didn't quite want the night to end so we settle on a diner. Long Island, NY is famous for terrific diners, with at least one in every town. You can get any kind of meal at any hour of the day or night, and the Kings Villa was one of the Island's best, in Carle Place, on the corner of Old Country and Glen Cove Roads. We drive over for coffee and talk at great length about all sorts of things.

Now if you knew Roseann personally, you'd know that in conversations with her it's a little tough to get a word in edgewise. I might run a close second, but I am now learning to "listen" a little better, so the conversation flows very nicely and a bit more evenly than usual. I realize, during our heart-to-heart that I miss the effervescence that is purely Roseann. The time flies by quickly, almost too quickly as she looks at her watch again, and realizes that she better get home. Her parents are loving, but understandably a little strict now about her curfew, and so we proceed back to her East Meadow neighborhood toward Clearmeadow Drive.

As we arrive and park my old, pale-gold Dodge Dart in front of her house, we can see her mother standing in the doorway. Roseann says she should go in. I surely understand her mom's concern, but I push the envelope just a bit and ask her to stay for a few minutes to say a prayer, and she agrees.

I feel I should try this listening prayer again and so I let Roseann know that I am going to try to just listen to God, and she readily says, "OK."

And so I listen.

Immediately the memory of the image of the throat comes to my mind. It distracts my prayer, so I try to push the thought out. It comes back again and I again attempt to banish it. It comes for the third time so I say, "Roseann, let me tell you what came to me in prayer this morning because it keeps coming back to me and maybe if I tell it to you, it will stop hounding me." And she answers again, "OK."

I tell her of how in prayer that morning, I saw, as clear as day, in my mind's eye, the inside of someone's throat and a flap of skin opening and closing. Instantly, a concerned, yet quizzical look comes across her face, and I simply ask, "What?"

And she slowly and carefully, as if speaking one word at a time replies, "When we were with Billy and Janet, and you were singing, I was trying to sing along with you…and I felt something like that in my throat." As she says this, her eyes lower as she touches the base of her neck in astonishment.

I look at her, beckoning her to raise her eyes, and then looking straight in those eyes and just as slowly, speak in as serious a tone as I thought appropriate, "Roseann…tomorrow morning…you go right to the doctor!"

I had never even suggested to anyone to go to the doctor in my entire life, but I never felt as strongly about anything I had ever said to anyone as I had in that moment.

I didn't hear the following events for two days after that evening. I was concerned for Roseann, but I was quite caught up in so many things, and I simply trusted she'd be ok.

And then I find out.

The next morning after our prayer together, Roseann asks her mother to bring her to the doctor. Even though she is now nineteen, she still has a pediatrician, and they are able to get an appointment with him early that morning. She is examined and he tells her that her throat is a little red, that she should take a pain reliever to call her in the morning if she feels any worse.

The moment they emerge from his office, Roseann tells her mother to take her to a specialist. Her mother responds, "You just saw the doctor and he said you were fine," but Roseann persists declaring, "Rob said that something was wrong…and I believe him."

They return home to look for a local ENT specialist and find the practice of Drs. Matucci and Kent in Great Neck. It would be a forty minute cab ride, as Marie never really drives out of the local area. She listens to her daughter, makes the immediate appointment and calls for the expensive Long Island cab, traversing the north shore of Long Island with a bit more fear and trepidation than on their morning trip.

After the doctor examines Roseann, he tells her, "Wait right here for a few minutes." He returns with a second doctor who also examines her. They briefly consult and one of them leaves the room only to return with a third doctor, who examines Roseann's throat as well. The three then look at each other and nod and the first one asks Roseann, "Are you here with anyone?" Roseann replies, "Well, my mother is in the lobby, but I'm nineteen-years-old, you can tell me." The doctor asks someone to get her mother.

When Marie enters the examination room, without delay the doctor says, "Your daughter has a granuloma, a little larger than a quarter, low in her throat. When she was intubated in the hospital, it must have scratched its inside, scar tissue had formed and a growth developed. Roseann needs to immediately go into the hospital for emergency surgery, if she doesn't, her air passageway will close within a day and she will surely suffocate."

Roseann is rushed to the hospital and emergency surgery is successfully performed. Her life is saved by a vital combination of prayer and medical science.

This awesome conclusion and new beginning for Roseann begins with a timely teaching of a cleric with a fervent heart and ends with an accurate and well-time medical evaluation and surgical procedure. And along the way, a number of us learn to listen… and to believe.

Another of Roseann's doctors after her accident had given her an overly, cautious prognosis. He had told her that she might not ever be able to bear children due to the severity of her injuries to her pelvis. As I write this day, thirty-eight years later, Roseann is the proud mother of two beautiful children. Joey is 30 years of age himself and stands at 6'2". Sarafina is 29, and the proud mother of three beautiful children of her own.

Upon Joey's birth in 1986, Roseann asked me if I would be his Godfather. Of course I accepted and will always have a special place for him and for Sara in my heart.

Roseann continues to talk up a blue streak to this day, albeit with a new story to tell. She has been and is a plentiful blessing to countless folks, young and old throughout her very blessed life.

I believe in God…and I believe in Roseann.

## Chapter Two

# Your Brother Daniel is Only One Step Away...

*I believe in God, and I believe in those He places in our way, whether they be seemingly good or difficult to deal with, easy to live with or hard. I believe that God is in all people and in all things, and that everything ultimately works out for the best when we turn things over to Him.*

Do you have someone in your life that you care about who may be going through some difficulties and is resistant to your help? Perhaps praying for and believing for them is really all you can do, and is actually the right thing.

About a year and a half prior to my experience with our friend Roseann, something great and wonderful happened within our own family. I have two brothers and two sisters, and at that time, all of us were living at home except for my older brother Danny.

Dan is then twenty-three-years-old and pretty much on his own. He manages a health club on Broadway in New York City and our family feels he might be becoming a little too caught up in the night life and all that the city offered. I am a true beginner in prayer at this time, and I so I entrust him into God's hands and believe on his conversion.

Over a six month period of time, I spoke with Dan two or three times about this new way of life I had found, but his response was always a slightly condescending, "That's great for you little brother, have a good time in church." His responses though didn't diminish my prayer for him. I feel a newfound responsibility for my family. What I had found...or really Who had found me...was too much of a gift to keep to myself.

One day my friend Tommy asks me to join him at an evening retreat. I had never been on any sort of retreat and I am excited to go. It is held on a Friday night in a small chapel in Roslyn, NY. Roslyn holds a warm place in my heart as the thought of it brings memories of childhood and Sunday visits to the duck pond where my brothers and sisters and I fed the ducks with our parents and sometimes grandparents and ate Mr. Softee Ice Cream.

The retreat is given by Father Vernard Poslusney, a gifted theologian, spiritual writer and Carmelite retreat director.

Father Vernard is seriously soft spoken, but his words hold a reverence and power unlike I had ever witnessed. One is taken with Father's apparent deep state of holiness as the small group of about twenty listens to him as he leads us in prayer. At one point he asks us all to kneel and to "listen" to our Lord; that God will speak to us individually. I do think it's a little presumptuous of him to say so, but I do as he asks. This is actually my first tangible experience in listening prayer and the request comes upon all of us in attendance suddenly, but very gently.

As I kneel and quiet my mind and heart I begin to just... listen, and within moments I hear something in my spirit that is near audible.

Clear as a bell, within my heart, I hear these words; "Your brother Daniel is only one step away."

Although I was excited for it, nothing that had been happening to me in my life at that point in time really surprised me; I was encountering just so many amazing things and I was just beginning to learn to ride this wave.

The next morning, I relay my encounter to my mother, who upon hearing what I tell her, quickly confirms the word. She had just returned from the Laundromat as our washer was on the fritz. She tells me of a teenager who shrieked just an hour before, "What has been lost has been found!" as he held the sock he had retrieved from the bottom of a dryer. She told me it immediately made her think of Danny.

One minute later, there goes that kitchen phone. I answer it. It is Dan. The first thing he says is, "Rob, I think I want to go to church with you." I then happily and humbly answer, "I know..."

We immediately make plans to meet at the Wine Gallery, a wine and cheese place in Forest Hills, Queens, just down the block from his apartment. We get together on Thursday night, and from the moment we arrive at the restaurant, I don't shut up. I begin to recount all of my experiences of the last several months. I so want Danny to experience the joy that had come into my life, but I still hadn't discovered yet, the genuine gift of listening.

I continue my diatribe in the car ride back to his place. We stay parked out front for at least another twenty minutes or so, and when I am finally talked out, Danny shakes his head and responds, "I don't know Rob, I just need more proof... I just need more proof."

With that, I look my brother square in the eye, slow my voice and say, "Danny...Sometimes God Works Just Like That," as I snap my fingers.

And as if on cue, the street lamp above our heads goes out right on the snap.

Danny turns white as even I could see in the blackened night and answers, "OK. I'll go to church with you."

The next week, I accompany Danny to Our Lady of Mercy Church Rectory to meet with Father Brassil. As we leave, Danny describes the half hour he spends with him. After hearing Dan's confession, Father prays over him.

Danny recounts to me his intense, spiritual experience and I can see it clearly leaves him in a sort of awe, his emotions touched deeply within him. After telling me, he is somewhat speechless during the rest of our car ride home as tears well up in his eyes and gently fall on his cheeks as he drives.

Within just a few weeks, he quits his job at the health spa and moves home. He spends the next year praying and studying the scriptures about every day.

It was during this time that I write my first song, and soon afterwards we begin our singing ministry. We are blessed over the next several years ministering in song to thousands of folks and enjoying the baby steps of our young Christian lives.

Danny moves on to have a brilliant career marketing Christian music as one of the top executives in the industry. He has met with world, business and spiritual leaders throughout his life and has enriched their lives as much as they have enriched his. God did have a very different plan for his life than he originally imagined, and you could say He Did it Just Like That.

I believe in God…and yeah, I believe in Dan.

## Chapter Three

# Ask and You Shall Receive... But a Van and Boots?

*So learning to listen...led to learning to believe... even more deeply.*

Have you ever had a hard time praying for temporal or physical things?

I recall my thoughts so vividly from this time in my life. I remember clearly as these events, big and small began to unfold, that I felt that the sky was the limit for belief. Yet, even with a college degree, I am still feeling my way as far as where my life will lead in terms of career. So I support myself taking part time jobs while trying to discover deeper meaning in life in general, and at the same time, wonder what direction my life will take. How could I not be intrigued by so great answers to prayer? And how could I also not logically believe that blessed experiences would surely follow in my relationship with the One who's Love I was really just beginning to encounter?

Yet my financial circumstance in those days was decidedly different from where it is today. I was, well…poor. As a husband and father of five today, I surely know and appreciate the financial struggles that many people have, but I'm not near as penniless now as in my early days of learning to believe.

My favorite Beatitude had become the first one, "Blessed are the poor in spirit, for theirs is the kingdom of Heaven."[2] But my poverty in my twenties wasn't spiritual. It was financial. Didn't have a pot… well, you know the rest.

At the close of one Friday night during our early Coffee House days, Dan and I are packing up our music equipment. We would always need to cram it into the trunk of our shared, old Ford Custom four-door. Not much room. Sometimes it requires two trips for the mile or so trek back home. As we pack up the amps and speakers this night, Dan blurts, "We need a van." I respond right away, "Okay, let's ask God for one."

Dan is becoming a man of faith, but his logical response is, "He's not going to give us a van!" To which I retort, "Why wouldn't He? We are doing His work and if we believe He can do all things, why not something as simple as a van?" So Dan agrees in prayer with me as we hold hands and thank God for the van that he would soon gift us with.

One week later, Danny is just outside of the Lamb's Club on West 44th Street in New York City that at the time is providing housing to local Christian musicians and artists. The housing is sponsored by the Church of the Nazarene.

2. Matthew 5:3

A relatively well known Christian Music duo, Mickey and Becky Moore arrive this morning in a let's call it, well-used Volkswagen Minibus. Danny introduces himself and then immediately says to Mickey, "Nice van!" Mickey answers, "Why do you say so?" Danny tells him of our prayer from the Friday night before. Mickey smiles and eagerly responds, "You want it? Becky and I just bought a new one to go out on tour with and were wondering what we were going to do with this one."

Gift graciously received.

We used that van for over two years shuttling equipment throughout the NY metropolitan area from coffee house to church to music festival until it finally died one, frigid night on the Southern State Parkway in Bellmore, NY. May it rest in peace.

The following winter, I am still taking odd jobs to support our ministry and it is starting to get a little cold. I realize that I don't have any boots for the sometimes freezing, northeast season approaching, and just don't have them in the budget. Recalling the van I pray silently and say, "Lord, I could use a pair of boots." I didn't recount this prayer to anyone. I kind of felt a little embarrassed even within myself. Although I was doing what I really believed to be God's work, I didn't have enough money to even buy myself a pair of boots. But I didn't question my faith; I just believed that in some way, God would provide.

This was among the fastest answers to prayer I had ever received and one of the most astonishing as well.

The very next day, someone who always seemed to struggle with his faith, my friend Vinnie, appears at our front door holding a pair of boots.

He sheepishly says, "Please don't think I'm crazy but the Lord told me to bring these to you. I thought it was pretty strange but I wanted to be obedient to what I thought was the Lord speaking to me."

Now I wear a size 11. These are only a 10, but I said, "Thanks" and kept my mouth shut. My feet were warm, yet squeezed a bit for the entire winter. Every time I placed them inside the worn leather of those tattered soles that season, I thanked God and believed in Him just a little bit more, step by step.

After I had thanked Vinnie, I told him of my prayer from the day before. I hope it helped his faith. He winced and looked at me kind of funny when I told him.

I believe in God…I believe in Vinny too.

## Chapter Four

# You Could Stop the President With That Rap...

*Time alone, if well spent, is extremely valuable in developing a sense of self, a sense of belief and a sense of God.*

Have you ever been literally astonished after a profound message has emerged for you?

I had never desired to spend any considerable amount of time alone, yet now eagerly looked forward to being by myself in prayer. The fruit of praying alone was that its joy couldn't keep me away from then wanting to be with and to share what I felt to be God's Love with others. Every day brought new and faith-building surprises; and all in such relative obscurity, yet I was feeling as if I was so protected... like in the palm of Someone's hand.

My prayer life was active and growing; my relationship with my God was beginning to find footing. For the first time in my life, on an every day basis, I felt fulfilled from the inside out, and I couldn't hold it in. Real, deep and profound love permeated my every day and night. I had never experienced anything at all quite like it. And so I took a job... driving a cab?

In 1978 there was little precedent for even moderately paid youth ministers in the Catholic Church; and that is what I was becoming, a youth minister, not even a paid one though. But truly, being compensated for the ministries I was a part of was the furthest thing from my mind. I really had no desire for money during those spiritually eye opening times. The intrinsic value of this new life, being wrapped up in what I felt so deeply as God's love, was what sustained me in my early years of my learning… to believe.

Many early twenty-something's, just starting out in life are just beginning to learn to believe in themselves. I really had little care in that type of occupation at that period in time. I was learning to believe in Someone much greater than myself, who I was also coming to believe...believed in me.

And so I began to drive a cab? My family's reaction was typical of what anyone's might be; relatively bright, young college graduate, not really attempting to pursue a career in the area of his studies, had them questioning my direction. I had graduated with honors with a degree in Communications in the media capitol of the world, and yet I had no desire to partake of what lied before me as the potential and seemingly obvious path to success.

Clearly, the humility would serve me well, and the simple lifestyle that year would afford me the freedom to continue to grow in a faith that would surely be a benefit in so many ways for so many years to come.

The first thing I began to realize was that cab drivers generally did not seem to experience a great deal of respect from many caught up in their own lives or careers. Don't get me wrong, many folks were nice, especially those of humble means, and there were many of those I would encounter, but by and large I didn't feel that I was really treated as a person, just as someone to take them from here to there. My prayer, as it was for everyone I met, was to be a help to take them from where they might be to who they might become.

In those days the scriptures about the wisdom of the simple confounding the wise would often sound in my ears.

If a door seemed to be open to conversation with a given fare I would always try to be ready. This was the case one day as I picked up and dropped off a young man in a relatively prevalent residential neighborhood on Long Island, New Castle.

He is about my age, maybe a little older. He seems a bit rough around the edges, yet is open and frank enough to ask why there is a Bible on my front seat. I readily share about some of the changes that are taking place in my life; he listens for the seven minute ride; I drop him off and I go on my way.

About a week or so later, I am dropping off a passenger not far from my own home in the early afternoon and decide to take some time for lunch and prayer. After my sandwich, I go to my room, read from scripture a passage about giving witness before kings and rulers and then promptly fall asleep.

After twenty minutes or so I awaken with another image in my mind's eye. I am barely awake, but the image is just as real, though different, as the one of Roseann's throat. It is of the face of President John F Kennedy.

It is as if it is an inner vision, but this time, there is an emotional connection for me. And why wouldn't there be? I was only ten years old when our president was assassinated, fifteen years before. I, like millions of Americans loved our president, although I had never dreamed of him before. But this isn't a dream.

As I don't quite understand it, I justify it as an immediate psychological response to the scripture I read just prior to falling asleep. This makes perfect sense.

No sooner do I reenter my dusty, yellow Checker Cab, does the raspy voice of my favorite dispatcher, Betty, blare through my two-way radio, "Robbit...you there?" I respond back, "Yeah Betty, watchu got?" Although a bit rough, her voice is usually lilting as if in sing song, "You got a pick up waitin for you at the Roosevelt Raceway," she tunes. "Check." I respond, as I start off for the five or so minute drive to the Westbury location.

Roosevelt Raceway, off of Old Country Road was a former trotter's race track, then being leased to a flea market a few days a week.

When I arrive, I pick up a young man who says he can't believe it is me. I think he says this because he might have recognized me from among the twenty or so drivers at the cab company, but he continues to eagerly try to engage me. I am still a little sleepy from my nap and prayer and really don't recognize him. He says excitedly, "You remember me from last week don't you"? I don't but don't say so; I am just trying to place his face as he continues to talk in rapid fire fashion. He beams, "I'm going to tell you what you did for me, alright? Do you know where you drove me last week? Seeming out of breath, he answers his own question. "You drove me to a prostitute's! You had no idea where you took me but there, right there on your front seat was your Bible and you started tellin' me about the Word and how God came into your life and all. What you didn't know was that my father-in-law is a pastor, my wife is saved and they've been prayin' for me for a long time. And you stopped me from goin' in that house! And you didn't even know any of that. I decided to let God in my life, right then and there!"

As I pull up to his home maybe ten minutes or so later, and as he exits my cab, he smiles widely, looks me in the eye and blares again to me, "You could stop the president with that rap you know; you could stop the president!"

I'm not quite sure about that, but I believe anything is possible for one... who believes.

I believe in God...I believe in that young man. I never got his name. I never saw him again, but have thought of him and have prayed for him and his family often. What a gift, to play a small part in helping a struggling, young husband to learn and then to decide...to believe.

## Chapter Five

# Bigfoot...

---

*Sometimes, singular graces are given just because they are needed.*

---

How can anyone discern the ways of God? Beats me!

Even though I do believe I have the gift... of believing, that doesn't mean that I understand it, or can even comprehend it. I often wonder why I don't always enjoy a more complete picture of certain circumstances or of life as a whole, but I think I am getting there... The more we learn and the more we grow, the more we realize how much we don't know. No matter, I think. The older I become, I kind of realize that learning to walk in faith is one of the more needed ingredients for a full and well balanced life.

On a sunny September Monday morning I was on the way back to the "rail." That's slang for the rail road station. This rail was in Westbury. I was driving down Post Avenue seemingly without a care in the world, just expecting a short break with the other cabbies as we would wait for the incoming 9:20 from Penn Station to arrive.

Just prior to turning down the back street behind the rails, I had as beautiful experience as I could remember. It was sudden, it was gentle, yet it was powerful. I felt as though I was being loved from outside of myself. And I was completely alone. My first thought was…"Well, look how much God loves me!" Yes, I was a novice to the ways of grace; I hadn't yet learned that there is a reason for everything.

So I pull up into the parking lot on the south side of the Westbury Train Station of the Long Island Rail Road, right along side a half dozen other cabbies, guys that I had come to know over the last few months. I really have to say they are a motley bunch as one might expect. But I have a deep respect for them. One is an immigrant with a thick polish accent, another, a biker dude with huge, tattooed biceps, long black hair, mustache and leather jacket. There is Rev, an older man who is a preacher from New Castle who needs to supplement his meager church income to support his family, and then… there is Bigfoot.

Bigfoot is nicknamed that because he wears a size 15 shoe. He is kind of an obnoxious young man of about 24. He projects as if he is full of himself, and if anything, the other cabbies I work with are relatively humble, so Bigfoot sticks out like a sore thumb in more ways than one.

No sooner than I had gotten settled, standing outside of the cab that clear morning does the conversation move quickly in an antagonistic direction. Bigfoot is getting the biker dude a little ticked off. The biker dude tells him to "Shut up!" Bigfoot is stubborn, and at this moment to me, seems to lack a little basic common sense, as he continues to bark back at the dude who looks like he might blow at any moment.

After a few more choice words, the dude warns him, to shut his mouth again, to which Bigfoot just puts his big foot right in it. Biker dude shouts, "That's it!" as he rushes to the back of his cab, and with purpose, opens its trunk and tightly grasps a tire iron with a crazed look in his eye. He begins to stomp towards Bigfoot.

And I reason to myself, "Ohhh..."

Without the slightest hesitation, I calmly slide in the position of Biker dude's face, with a genuine and wide smile on my own and say, "You really don't want to do this," to which he fumes, "Get away, I'm gonna #!%## kill that #@!!%# son of ##@!%."

And still smiling, I very evenly answer, "And If you do... you'll be in jail tonight and for a lot longer too." He glares at me, still crazed, then slows, then slams the tire iron down as it clangs on the pavement and barks, "Well, make sure that @#%&@ stays away from me."

I think Bigfoot finally got the message.

Now I am the type of guy that will always try to help anyone in need if I am able. And even without the whoosh of love I had just experienced, I may have tried to help in that situation. But my level of maturity at that point in time would probably have led me to yelling at the both of them, and when I think about it, that would most likely have exacerbated the situation. The only thing on my mind though, when the dude went at Bigfoot, was that explosion of grace I had received a mere five minutes before. I had instantly realized that the gift… was not for me… it was for the biker dude and for Bigfoot.

I was glad that I was driving a cab that day. I believe in God…and I believe in cabbies… we are people too.

## Chapter Six

# Will I Live a Long Life?

---

*Don't ignore your intuition. Try to go with it…*
*it's the only way you'll sharpen it.*

---

How long are you going to live?

Hey, there comes a time or times for all of us when we are faced with the thought of our own mortality. By God's grace up until this time in my life, I had never really faced a serious illness of my own. But on a day in 1979, for the first time ever, as a 25-year-old, I thought about it.

I awoke that morning with a single notion on my mind, "I could get hit by a truck!" Kind of a funny thought to wake up to, but seriously, I had never considered dying even once up until that day. I guess most young people don't. When we are young, that is, I imagine the furthest thing from our minds. But this day it is my first thought.

And so, I pray. And I pray these same words exactly and immediately.

"God, will I live a long life?"

And you know, it was the ONLY prayer I prayed the entire day. Now I don't recall anything else of that particular day except its beginning and its ending, but have carried it's blessing with me throughout my entire life.

I do remember deciding to end my day early, intending to retire at just before 11 pm. I would ordinarily go to bed between midnight and 1 am and didn't necessarily feel any more tired than usual, but just plain decided to go to bed early.

On my parent's kitchen table, my mom had an inspirational centerpiece. It was a small, plastic replica of a loaf of bread with the raised words imprinted on it "The Bread of Life." And there was a cutout in the top of it holding maybe 40 small rectangular, pastel-colored cards. And on each card there was a scripture verse with corresponding prose on its reverse side.

And so I pick out one, light green card and this is what it says,

"With long life I will bless thee…"[3]

I have never given any further thought to what the length my life will be. This I know is a special gift to me. Never did I question this before that day, nor had I ever prayed a prayer regarding it, except for that day; and the only scripture verse I read the entire day answered the only prayer that came from my lips.

I believe in God. And I believe in His Living Word.

---

3. Psalm 91:16

## Chapter Seven

# Papa...

*Always be open to new friends of any and every age...*
*and do your best to cherish them.*

Do you believe that sometimes earthly friends are sometimes heaven sent?

There are not many people that I believe have had as much of an impact on my life as did one old soul with a special twinkle in his eyes.

I was to move on from my job driving a taxicab to one driving another segment of the population...senior citizens.

My friend Tommy, always seeming to be a catalyst for me, let me know that Catholic Charities was hiring. The job entailed driving seniors to a lunch program. Still, it had nothing to do with my degree, but I felt in my heart, that there would be something to this sort of ministry that would serve me well as I continued to begin my adult life...and I was correct.

The job was pretty simple. It consisted of taking one or two daily runs in an oversized, passenger van through the towns of Farmingdale, Massapequa and Massapequa Park on Long Island. I would pick up senior citizens and bring them to a lunch program, serve them and then drive them back home. The program itself was a pretty cool way of life for those over sixty-five, who could for a dollar, enjoy a complete, hot lunch and join in a morning and early afternoon of friendship.

There were so many characters at St. Luke's and it was a joy to be a part of their lives for a little over a year. Although just twenty-five, I really took to becoming a part of their daily routines and strived to learn from those that had so much valuable life experience to share. Each had his or her own cadence and rhythm and some had personalities that would just beat the barn, and so every day held its own special reward. I was learning to just live in the moment, and I was surrounded by so many great teachers.

Although I learned from these many, I am especially drawn to one that everyone calls Papa.

The reason for his beloved moniker is because he is old enough to be the father of really any of them, and wise and loving enough that all would seek to be under his wing.

He is married to Mama, twelve years his junior at eighty-five. Papa is gentle, soft spoken, and aware of everyone and everything around him. Mama would joke that "Papa has many girlfriends" and he would smile; because all of the girls just love Papa. All of the men respect him. He has a stately, but very soft appearance and his 5'9" stature, seems a mere reflection of a man who would have been much taller in his physical prime. But his spiritual height is clearly the most evident aspect of his persona, and I would learn, few could come close to reaching his elevation.

At the last stop on my second run most mornings, I would greet him, "Good Morning, Papa!" And with his warm smile he would respond cordially, "Good Morning, Bob!" He was the only person I felt comfortable calling me Bob. I've been Rob as long as I can remember, except as a boy when I was Robbie. But Papa could call me anything he wanted; I grew to love and respect him so.

My experience at Catholic Charities began on a positive note every day that year, except for one.

For whatever reason, my boss, Marlene, a woman usually with a relatively positive and somewhat spiritual outlook, accused me of stealing $36.00 from the seniors and lying about it. Now I thought it was quite laughable to be charged with such an offense as there would be no reason I would want or need to steal such a sum. One of the reasons I was even working there was that money held really little importance to me. So I calmly answer her, that I didn't steal any money. I expect her to then likely change her tune, but she gets a little angry that I was disagreeing with her and so she points her finger at me and calls me a liar!

Well, I was raised to be a gentleman, so smiling, I again calmly and quietly say that she must have been misinformed but I did not steal anything nor am I lying. She immediately becomes very agitated, her face turns beet red, she raises her voice even louder, and blurts, "You stole that $36.00!!!"

Now I was not really angry. I kind of thought it was a little funny, but I figured that since my calm attitude did nothing but anger her further, another course of action might be appropriate. So I stand up, take the clipboard I am holding, slam it on my desk and shout myself, "I DID NOT LIE AND I DID NOT STEAL!"

Well, I hadn't realized that this would scare the heck out of her. I am 6 foot tall and she is about 5' 3". I immediately discern that she feels threatened so I pick up my clip board and quietly, yet very quickly leave the office to begin my morning runs.

And I feel terribly. I hadn't been angry with her but I feel badly that I scared her, no matter how ridiculous her accusations had been. I was not used to scaring people, especially women. So I am quieter than usual that morning as I pick up my seniors.

When I arrive on Papa's doorstep, I still greet him, "Good Morning, Papa." And he responds as always, "Good Morning, Bob!" I smile at him, and as usual, slowly accompany him to the van, help him up and in, and then a little more quietly than is customary for me, drive the quarter mile back to St. Luke's.

As always I help Papa off the van and into his wheel chair. He could certainly walk, but not unaided and not more than maybe a dozen steps at a time. I wheel Papa into the hallway as I always do and then go back outside to pull the van into its spot.

Every morning, one of the sprier woman elders would wheel Papa from the hallway into one of the classrooms where many of the seniors would gather while they waited for lunch. I recall the sense of pride she felt in fulfilling her special, morning duty. When I arrive back in the building, less than one minute after leaving Papa, he is still in the hallway. I immediately think, "How strange! Why would Papa still be here?" He had never been left there before.

As I approach, he looks deep into my eyes in a loving way—he seemed to have no other—and says, "Bob, come here." As I move closer and look to him to listen he says, "No, come down here," motioning that I should at least stoop down to the level of his chair.

My respect of Papa has me stoop, then squat down to just below his level as I wait to listen to what he wants to tell me. I feel like a little boy. I have no clue what he is about to say.

He motions to me with his index finger to wait. He then closes his eyes, tilts his head slightly, places three fingers over his lips and seems to begin to go into a deep thought. Just ten seconds later, his eyes still closed, he nods, then turns his head back towards me, opens his eyes and speaks...

"When I was in World War I, one of my fellow sailors came into the barracks and accused me of lying and stealing!"

I haltingly ask, "What did you do?"

Papa mimics the action of slowly making a fist, with a slightly astonished look on his own face at what he had done and with his thick German accent answers, "I hit him in the mouth!"

"My superior officer comes in and asks, 'What is that man doing lying in the corner?' 'I hit him,' I said, to which the officer responds, 'To the brig with you...thirty days...bread and water.' "

Looking downward he pauses and then says as his voice trails off, "Ten days later… my submarine went out to sea…and never returned."

The entire crew of the U Boat that Papa would have been on, had he not been in the military jail, was lost at sea.

And here is Papa, sixty-two years later, relaying this story to me, of how he lost his temper so long ago, on the only day that I unnerved my boss, in a strikingly similar way.

I looked up at Papa…and I believed.

And yes, my perspective shifted as I walked down the hallway to return my clipboard to the office and quietly prepare to serve lunch. I didn't feel quite so guilty anymore that I frightened Marlene, realizing she should quickly get over it. I surely wouldn't make her day any more difficult than it had started. But I was so deeply impressed by this great man of God. How could he possibly have known what had been on my mind that morning? Had someone in that one minute I was pulling the van into its nearby parking space told him what I had experienced with my boss? Unlikely I thought, but possible.

But some other occurrences with my friend told me otherwise. This wasn't my only unusual experience with Papa.

A few weeks later, I had heard thrice in a short period of time that too much sugar was not really good for you. I had no weight problem, always being rather slim up until that time in my life, yet I heard on the radio, on TV and in a magazine article of the harmful effects of too much sugar. So I awoke this particular day resolved to lessen my sugar intake.

It was lunch time at St. Luke's. I had picked up about sixteen seniors that morning. One of the benefits of the job was that I could partake of the $1 lunch if I wanted to and most often I did. Lunch that day was roasted chicken breast, green beans and sweet potato.

Papa is sitting in his usual section in the auditorium already at work at his weekday feast. I am seated with some of my fellow workers a little more than twenty yards away, there being several rows of tables between Papa and me.

As I approach my sweet potato, I pause and think to myself, "Should I eat this? There's sugar in it." And then I immediately realize that those sugars would be natural so that wouldn't be such a bad thing. And then I kind of chuckle on the inside thinking what a foolish thing to be concerned about. I promptly cut my sweet potato in two and compromising with my thought, eat only half.

After lunch, when the seniors had departed down the long hallway to the waiting rooms I would join my partner and other driver Bill and put away the cafeteria tables and chairs. This was about a twenty-minute process. Upon finishing the tables this day, I enter the hallway by myself and there is Papa, sitting in his wheel chair, again alone and waiting for me.

He says, “Bob…” pausing greatly giving me time to approach him. With that twinkle in his eyes he offers…"You can have sweet potatoes..."

I had no response for him.

I had been told that Papa sat in the same seat every Sunday morning in his Lutheran church for longer than anyone could remember. His occupation in the states until his retirement many years before was owner of a typewriter repair shop. He loved Mama. He walked slowly, everyone loved and respected him and he was my friend. There were seventy-two years between our ages and that didn't seem to matter at all to either of us.

These experiences with Papa were not my most profound. Those would come a little later.

One morning, my boss tells me that she has some sad news. She said that Papa is in the hospital and it doesn't look like he is going to make it. I thank her immediately and then run to the pay phone. I put my thirty-five cents in and call the Our Lady of Mercy Rectory and ask for Father Brassil. Father is not in, and so I leave a message for him to go to Central General Hospital in Plainview to visit and pray with patient Herman Hoffman.

About two weeks later, Marlene tells me first thing that she has good news. Papa is coming back today. He has made a remarkable recovery.

I drive to Cherry Street that morning and greet Papa and Mama as usual, “Good Morning, Papa!” I beam. “Good Morning, Bob!”

He responds. Mama does her best to teeter passed us and I slowly walk Papa down the crooked, slate steps of his front lawn and onto and into the van. We walk a little slower this morning... and it is a warm reunion.

We are about two thirds of the way through the short trip to St. Luke's when Papa catches his breath and calls out to me from his usual seat directly behind mine. "Bob...That Father Brassil.... Nice young man." I smile. Father was in his fifties.

Papa was notably slowed over the next few months, but we were all blessed with his continual presence and I will never forget his smile, his gentleness, the example he set of what it was to be someone... who believed.

And so one Monday morning, my boss Marlene tells me she has some sad news again. Papa's health has deteriorated and he is back in the hospital. And something inside me says...OK.

I don't run to the phone. Papa is 97½ years old. He had lived a beautiful and charmed life. He has had a tremendous and quiet impact on the lives of so many, and his last years are among his best. I feel I shouldn't interfere with what appears to be this final stage of his life.

I finish my runs that morning feeling a gentle resolve. After that last trip, as I arrive in the kitchen to see what we are having for lunch, Marlene asks me to be "meals on wheels" for one of the seniors, Mary from Massapequa Park, who doesn't quite feel up to coming in. I readily agree, take the small cooler and hop up into the van for the ten minute drive.

I think about Papa on the way, and begin to pray for him on the way back to St. Lukes. At that time in my life, most of my prayer, except for prayer at Mass, was internal. But for some reason I began to quietly pray out loud. I was of course alone in the van driving, so I didn't fear that anyone would hear or see me speaking all by myself.

And so I pray, "Thank you God for Papa. Thank you for the witness of his life. Thank you for his friendship. Thank you for everything good about his life." I felt so blessed to have been a small part at the end of his life and blessed to have learned so much about how to live this life from him.

And as I begin to pray, my prayers get louder. I feel kind of strange because I am not really a preacher, having never really reached this particular level of volume praying before. And I'm not feeling over emotional; it's just that my prayer gets loud. And I begin near shouting Alleluias… and it is really cool. I feel a great amount of inner peace and joy.

I reach St. Luke's. Lunch is about finished; I hurriedly eat mine, put the tables away, drive the seniors home and go home myself.

The next morning on my arrival to the office, Marlene says that she has sad news. Papa has passed. But she says that there is something she thinks I should know.

Papa had actually been in a coma since the prior Friday. And she recounts, "Yesterday, he awoke from his coma. At his side were Mama, his daughter Lottie and son-In-law Walter and his Pastor. He looked into Mama's eyes and told her, "The Lord is calling me home. Soon He will call you too. You are to stay in my home. Don't go live with Lottie. (Lottie and Walter lived just a few doors down on Cherry Street as well.) Stay in my home until the Lord calls you home too."

He then looked at his pastor, smiled one last time at Mama, closed his eyes and died.

I ask Marlene, "Do you know about what time yesterday this was?" And she replies, "Yes. It was just a little after noon."

Those were the exact moments I was praying aloud in the van, thinking I was all by myself.

It was a gift to be able to reflect on my friendship with Papa so often over the next several years, and really throughout my life. My place in our band Morningstar afforded me the opportunity to share this story with countless people. The music we wrote and shared often seemed to soften hearts and that, I believe, is so necessary to opening a person to higher truths than they might not have presently held. I wrote this song as a tribute to Papa's life which was so long and so blessed, and his death which also taught me things I would not have known had I not been a part of the amazing experience of his life.

## "Papa"

"...Good Mornin' Papa...Good Mornin' Mama too,
Good Mornin' Papa...You know that I love you

He died the first of February...a clear cold winter's day
We had been praying for some time...I didn't know what to say
He'd been on earth a few years...bout 97 ½
Some old and then some new years...but he walked a narrow path

Good Mornin' Papa...Good Mornin' Mama too,
Good Mornin' Papa...You know that I love you

It's a shame that still some folks say...it's over now he's gone

Cause I just get the feeling that his memory lingers on
His smile, O so gentle...his handshake it was warm
In his eyes I could see Jesus...in his heart there was his song.

His song it spoke of Mama...his wife of sixty years
I could see her at his funeral...her eyes so full of tears
And they flowed just like a river...in witness of his love
Some day soon he'll be with her
Forever home above

Good Mornin' Papa...Good Mornin' Mama too,
Good Mornin' Papa...You know that I love you

She knew how to be blessed by him...to prepare her last few years
Cause right before he died...he calmed her of her fears

He said, 'Mama He calls me...our Savior calls me home
And now until He calls you...you live and pray in our home.'

And now my Mama's happy, she says. "So long as you believe
the Lord He will be with you."...And He will never leave.

Good Mornin' Mama, Good Mornin' Papa too.
Good Mornin' Mama...You know that I love you."

I believe in God. And I believe in Papa. Good Mornin' Papa.
(Good Mornin' Bob)

## Chapter Eight

# Higher are His Ways...

*It is true that we can use our power of unbelief to stifle wonderful things from happening. But even in our unbelief God can do and does great things.*

Have you ever been somewhat wrong at a time when you were convinced... that you were right?

I felt somewhat surrounded during these times in the late seventies with an awareness of a growing movement of prayer, belief, healings of all sorts, folks being healed of emotional, spiritual and yes even physical ailments. There is significant scientific research that seems to prove the value of belief in the healing process and we are truly just at the beginning of our understanding of the ways of prayer and belief.

Spending much of my time almost exclusively with seniors, just during that one year or so, taught me an awful lot about human behavior. Because I was welcomed so readily by over a hundred seniors of all ages, races and creeds I was able to get to know many of them closely, their hopes and even their fears.

I walked many of them to and from their homes for short, slow trips and some would readily confide in me. I felt so honored to be in such a position to possibly be of help. I was a young, strong, growing man of faith and I felt I had much to offer them as well.

One afternoon I was beginning to walk Louise up the steps to the home she shared with her daughter's family on Sullivan Street in Farmingdale. Louise had been stricken with Polio as a child and as a sixty eight-year-old, still walked with a leg brace and a cane strapped to her arm for support. Her gait was decidedly uneven, and one could not but feel a deep compassion for her in her every challenged step. I always needed to take extra, special precautions with her over curbs and steps.

Louise was sometimes irreverent but certainly not by today's standards. I had a special love for her as our seeming different cultures and points of view collided on more than one occasion during the thirty minutes or so we spent together each day with the other seniors on the trips to and from the center.

But this one May afternoon, as soon as she and I exit the van and we are safely away from earshot of the other seniors, she tugs sharply at my arm while we walk to quietly tell me something. A look of fear comes across her face as she asks me to pray for her. She pleads, just like a little girl would, "Bobby, I'm scared." Then seeming embarrassed to tell me that she had a growth on her back, she confides that she is going to the doctor in the morning to have it removed. She implores, "Would you please pray for me?"

I gently stop in our tracks, and pray with her right then and there. I very lightly place my hand over her clothing and the spot on her upper back where the growth is, but not touching it at all. I pray, "Lord, please give Louise peace as you bless her doctor's hands to do all he can as he operates on her. Please help Louise to know that You are with her as she undergoes the procedure and make it all turn out the best way possible."

We then finish our measured walk up the steps; she smiles at me, still quite nervously though, and goes in the house.

Two days later, Louise is on my list of morning pick-ups. When I arrive on her front stoop, she has already seen me coming and for the first time ever, she is already out of her front door, and locking it behind her.

Louise turns to me and tells me right away that she is OK. She reports that it was a good thing I prayed, as she takes my arm and we begin to descend her cement steps. Thinking that it must have been a minor procedure and that Louise probably had been overreacting to her impending surgery I ask if the doctor felt that he got the entire cyst. She says, "Ohhh no...As soon as I went in the house after you prayed…it fell off my back. I didn't need the surgery," as she stops and straightens as much as she is able. She is standing proudly as if to communicate that she had claimed her healing and that God had taken care of her.

Up until that time, no one had ever asked me to pray for a cyst before. God had a different answer than what I had asked for.

I really didn't understand these types of things as they began to unfold during my life and I really don't totally understand them today, just that I believe that God does truly love us and wants the best for us. But I began to share these experiences with family and friends and then more folks began asking me and my family for prayer. From about that time onward, we always tried to pray as soon as we were asked, and do so up until this day.

There have though become times where I kind of felt that folks put more emphasis on me and my family than they did on God and that would sometimes bother me.

Mother Angelica once told me and my family that we are all just dodos for the Lord. It seemed like she felt it was her solemn duty to tell us that we should just let Him do what He wants with us. Recalling that makes me laugh to this day, but it was probably the best advice I had ever been given, grounding me in the humility that successful prayer rightly requires.

That didn't mean that sometimes I would not grow weary with prayer requests. One Friday night, just prior to our band ministering at the Catacombs Coffee House at St. Christopher's Church in Baldwin, NY, my young friend, Jane asks me to pray for a fellow teenage girl who came for the first time. I had recently been growing a bit tired of folks depending on my family and me for prayer as I knew that God hears and answers everyone's prayers. So I gently, yet curtly tell her that someone else can pray for her. She then grabs my arm and physically pulls me across the floor to the young girl.

When I arrive at the corner of the room, the girl is sitting quietly by herself and she explains to me that she has a lump on the side of her neck and asks me to pray over it.

I feel horrible for her. She is maybe seventeen, innocent and visibly afraid, way too young I think to have such a malady. But at the same time, I also really believe that someone else is supposed to do the praying that night, not me. How can I not pray though? It would be terribly cruel to deliver what I believe to be my discernment and then to just walk away. I would not be able to live with myself. And so recalling and reciting a passage from the Letter of St. James, I pray with her, even though, in my heart, I truly believe that this prayer is someone else' responsibility. My belief, in my estimation is truly not at play here.

For whatever reason, the next three months for me were very difficult spiritually. No matter what I seemed to try, my avid prayer life of a few years seemed to have finally dried up. I still went to church maybe twice a week, read the Bible and prayed as much as I could, but just didn't feel nearly as joyful as I had for such a long period of time.

But we continued our ministry and then, on another Friday night, Morningstar is booked at the new location of the Catacombs, at the north end of Baldwin. Right before we go on, a peaceful-looking, young, teenage girl approaches me. I don't recognize her but she identifies herself as the same girl that I prayed with three months prior, the one with the lump on the side of her neck.

She then tells me that when she woke up the very next morning, the lump had disappeared. She went to her same doctor. He examined and tested her thoroughly, and all he could do was to pronounce a total and inexplicable healing.

As nicely as I could, I asked her that if she ever has an answer to such a prayer again, to maybe let the person who prayed with her know as soon as she is able. I didn't tell her that I had a rough three months and it might have helped my own faith if she had somehow sought me out to let me know. Her telling me though did renew my faith, and deep joy in my prayer life returned almost immediately.

And these types of spontaneous healings are truly extraordinary gifts. But are they really? Might they, if we spent more conscious effort developing our gift of believing, take place much more often?

I believe they would.

Yet, I am more interested in the small, daily healings that we can bring to others in our every day lives; a look of love, patience with a family member, friend or stranger who may just need an ear or a moment of our time. True healing can take place every day in so many ways if we just take the time to express our God given presence to others, even when we believe it is not the most ideal time for us.

I shared a song that night at St. Christopher's, one that I had sung many times before. I wrote it during a day of personal prayer, a day where I had really the whole day to myself, a day when I was able to listen…to feel… and to believe.

## The Love of God

I have something I'd like to share…that I just can't describe
It's the Love of God
I've got such a sweet, sweet feeling inside
It's the Love of God

Did you ever see a kid with a secret…just about to burst open wide?
Well I feel like that kid with that secret…I've got God on my side

Did you ever feel that you were not really alone…
that someone was watchin' over you?
Wouldn't you always like to feel right at home?
Well I'm sure that's what Jesus wants for you

Don't you just wanna take off and fly…
past the clouds to the stars in the sky?
To live free and never die
You can with God on your side.

I know I've read it time and again
That sometimes when Jesus spoke
Some listened and stayed…but some walked away
But today…I have a special prayer of hope
That for once we all will listen…
as He stands at our door knocking
Our hearts He wants to christen… And to fill our stocking

I just remembered what else He said,
that if two or more ask anything in His Name
Then it will be done by His Father who is in heaven
So I ask…us now to pray the same

Isn't it great to just take off and fly
Past the clouds to the Lord in the sky
To live free...and never die
With the Lord on our side.

I know it's something that I just still can't describe
I mean...the Love of God
Except for a sweet, sweet feeling inside
Yes...it's the Love of God
Oooh the Love of God...Oooh the Love of God

I cannot answer those who contend that God could not exist because of all of the suffering and evils of this world. In the same way, I cannot fully understand the manifestations of believing, and the great examples of caring that our world has wrought and which are happening in this very moment.

I just believe in God, I believe in prayer and I believe in you.

## Chapter Nine

# Morningstar...

---

*Being open to continual conversion opens one up to deep internal and external adventures.*

---

Are you blessed enough to have found what life is truly calling you to…at least for the moment?

Our music ministry was spiritually thriving. Dan and I were joined by Frankie, then Joe and then Larry. Morningstar was booked almost every weekend for some coffee house, prayer service or music festival in the New York metropolitan area, and we joined with other young musicians in what seemed like a never ending blessing for about three years. We helped other parishes and other denominations open weekly coffee houses in their own churches and to say it was a fulfilling time in our lives would not do it justice.

We were becoming relatively well known in church circles, yet that was never our focus. We felt compelled to share the Love of

God and that's what we did. We were certainly aware of many of our own faults and weaknesses, but being young and single and becoming single minded in our faith, we were unencumbered and freely moved in the Spirit that we could call our own.

What was veritably unique in our band was the charism of being able to blend our completely different musical styles and personalities into a cohesive sound and ministry. We were all as different as night and day, yet with God's grace, and egos aside we were able to express God's message of love and bring so many to a deeper experience of presence, joy and faith.

Yet as rapidly and as powerfully as our joint union formed, just as quickly we began to disperse. We were of course, young men each looking towards our own futures. Dan became engaged to Janet, Frankie to Rose, and Joe was off to his own ministry, leaving Larry and myself to carry on the torch of Morningstar. We did so eagerly and prayerfully.

An odd pair, Larry and me. The first time we met neither of us liked the other, and yet he became, and is to this day, one of my most trusted friends and advisors. At this writing, Larry is still a youth minister, actually the campus minister and Theology chair at St. Mary's High School in Manhasset, NY. He has counseled thousands of teens over decades as their friend and mentor in his unique and unabashed style of sharing the Gospel.

But again, in 1979 it was just the two of us as the sole representatives of Morningstar. It was such a joy to minister with such an enthusiastic convert and accomplished musician.

Larry's conversion was certainly unique. He had been a rocker. He held a music degree from Five Towns College and was the front man for the 50s band, The Dukes, who at that time were among the most renown revival groups in the New York metropolitan area.

He had been led to St. Christopher's Teen and Young Adult Group by a few friends and eagerly attended these Friday night coffee houses for one reason. The girls were not only cute, but their custom of greeting every visitor with a hug and holy kiss was too much for this young man to pass up. Why wouldn't he feel at home, surrounded by bright, young girls who offered what he considered to be flattering attention?

Not that he wasn't used to that, he enjoyed a lot of adulation in the clubs as he fronted for the pumped up Rock band. But there was something so much more wholesome and loving about these young women that made it next to impossible for him to stay away.

And so, after a number of weeks, his male friends who had introduced him to the fellowship, grew a little weary of Larry's concentration on the girls. They urged him to read the Bible. They handed him a copy of the "Good News" and Larry agreed to read it.

Now Larry was of Jewish descent, and his mother was a Unitarian, although neither of his parents raised him with any particular faith. They also had both died when he was a teenager, and he, his sister and brother were then raised by his grandparents.

This night when Larry got home, he did read from the Bible. He read the entire Gospel of Matthew and then went to sleep. To this day, he can't explain it, but he tells often that when he awoke, he just believed… in God. Never had up until that day, and has never waivered since. He was just filled with a knowing that God existed and that God loved him personally.

Larry was so important to me at that time in my life and ministry, as the other lads were fulfilling their own dreams of beginning their families and I had yet more to do and to learn. And now I had a good friend with similar gifts and similar dreams. We sang and played together for several years and were told by many that their faith was strengthened through our music. Larry often told me that my song, "Five Years Old" was one that helped to remind him to believe, when life presented its special challenges

## Five Years Old

Lord, I remember when I was only 5 years old
then I told you that I loved You
And I was living, in Your Spirit even then, then I was a child of God
But through the years, I'd drift away from Your Love
Falling into a life of greed, lust and hate
They said there was no real God up above
And I would die, to accept my fate

Lord I remember when I was just a little kid,
and my heart sang to you gently
And when I fell down, I would get back up again, cry a little
and You'd console me
But over the years I seemed to forget Your consolation
The Truth that You taught me, in such a simple lesson
Oh but life had become, one large complication
And all cause I left the side of Your only Son

Lord I remember like it was only yesterday,
life in my soul, love and good times
I felt so special, in knowing all your love for me
that I cried real tears of joy
But all of those tears turned to anguish and despair
Filled once with love, then I was torn by my fear
I had fallen so low trying to climb to the top
I cried out in pain, thinking that no one was near

Lord I remember when I was only 5 years old,
then I told You, that I loved You
And when I fell down, I would get back up again, cry a little,
and You'd console me

Now I see my Lord, that it's the lesson of my life
When I fall down, You will pick me up again.
Your hand is tremendous, but as soft as the wings of Your Dove
With Your Love ever endless, You will always be my friend
Lord You know I feel like, I am only 5 years old..."

I believe in God…and to this day, I believe in Larry.

## Chapter Ten

# A Little Miracle…

*Miracles are all around us.*
*We need just open our eyes.*

What do you believe in?

The more I was integrated into church life, the more fearless I kind of became. I was not so afraid of what people would think about me, I was more preoccupied with learning what it meant to be in God's will… in the moment.

It wasn't unusual for me at that time to receive phone calls from folks with sometimes serious needs. Because I was relatively unencumbered, I was usually able to readily respond to these types of requests. I truly wanted to help and to become all that I believed God was trying to help me to be.

It is that way one very crisp, cold night in late January.

My friend John calls and his voice is much more serious than usual. It is a grave situation. He tells me that his infant nephew has been stricken with spinal meningitis. He is at the Nassau County Medical Center, the same hospital that Roseann had been in. He asks me to come and there is no question I would do so right away.

When I arrive some twenty minutes later, I am quietly greeted by John, his brother-in-law who is the father of the baby and John's Dad the baby's grandfather in the pediatric wing of the hospital. Because such close relatives of the baby are present to pray, I don't really feel that my presence is significantly important yet I surely understand the magnitude of the situation and the real and true need for joining in prayer.

I am perennially astounded by the great strides in science and have such high regard for medicine and psychology as disciplines. But I also believe in something much higher and have experienced the inexplicable so many times when it comes to exercising the simple gift… of believing.

And so many times it had more to do with others belief than with mine. I was asked by these men to join them in the recitation of the Rosary.

At that early time in my prayer life, the Rosary was not an important part of my routine. For whatever reason I could not easily relate to prayer with the Blessed Mother of God. I was still getting my feet wet in believing in and trying to understand the Eternal Trinity, than to spend any considerable amount of time in other types of prayer that I did not necessarily feel called to. Yes, I was a Catholic, yet my thought was, "If my prayer life ain't broke, don't fix it."

Yet I certainly respect their desire to pray, their devotion, and the seriousness of the situation. And who am I to intrude on their deep beliefs?

And so there we kneel, on the 19th floor in the reflection of floor-to-ceiling windows surrounding us, with miles of visible skylight, praying the Rosary for John's baby nephew.

We pray the whole Rosary. As we do, I entreat the Holy Spirit of God to pour out his compassion on this young father and his only son.

When we finish, we speak about the wonders that we have experienced over the last several years. I do my best to believe on a miracle for this devout family in their time of need.

And so it happens. After an hour, the baby's doctor comes into the waiting room to summon the baby's father. He faces him and says directly to him, "Please come with me."

He is not three or four strides in front of us as they walk towards the single bed unit when he turns again and says, "I don't know what religion you guys are, but this baby had spinal meningitis and now there's no trace of it, I think that you all should come."

We couldn't believe our ears. After one recitation of the Rosary, and I'm sure countless pleas of others, our prayers were readily answered.

My thoughts in that moment were threefold. First that the witness that we four gave, on our knees in a public place was honored by our God. And then, that it may have been mere coincidence, or that perhaps the baby's condition may have originally been misdiagnosed.

My uncertainty about this apparent answer to prayer lingered for a few years with me. That is, until something that happened at another time, in another place helped me to find the connection with another's gift…of believing.

I believe in God…And I believe he hears and cares for our every prayer. Sometimes the answer is no, often, the answer is not yet, and sometimes the answer is a resounding YES.

## Chapter Eleven

# Full Time Youth Ministry...

*Don't look for signs, but you can expect them.*
*And heed them when they come.*

Where are you being called today?

I was now four years into my discovery of my faith and my quest to find out what the heck I was going to do with the rest of my life. Yes it was a whirlwind, but boy was it confusing at times. All of my college friends are now well into their careers, accountants, television executives and architects, all on the fast track to success. And where was I? I was driving a van, taking senior citizens to lunch and working part time as a non-paid Youth Minister. Yes, I absolutely loved my life, but it lacked a certain traditional cohesiveness and structure. I had this inner sense though, that I may have been more in the right place than any of the friends I had gone to school with. And the fruit of my meanderings, deep love, abiding peace and sometimes intense joy was what continued to egg me on to new, albeit unusual adventures.

And then it happened…a shot at legitimacy.

My own Church was growing in her understanding of the need to reach out more concretely to young people. The Catholic Church was to offer full time positions for Youth Ministers, and they would be paid positions. It was what I had been hoping for. It would be the perfect next step for me.

And so I applied. And then I was directly disappointed.

I filled out the detailed application, noting my four years experiences in two parishes and my music ministry. I took the required psychological profile, which I was happy to pass. And then came an in depth interview. I was forthright and I was comprehensive in my answers and I felt that it went about as well as it could have gone.

And then came the hammer. The director of the program calls me a few days later and he tells me that I am over qualified for the job, that they are looking for kids right out of college to fill these positions. Yet he straight away offers me another job. My diocese, the Diocese of Rockville Centre, NY was affiliated with the North East Center for Youth Ministry and I am being offered a job to replace two people in the Diocese of Scranton, PA.

I think to myself, "You've got to be kidding me!!! I've spent four years serving my Church on Long Island without pay, my ministry with Morningstar is highly successful, I feel I am loved and supported by many, and you are asking me to move to Scranton? How do you not realize that my gifts and my ministry are here???"

I breathe...and politely answer that I don't think that is what I am called to do. He asks me to think about it and I agree I will, but in my heart, there is nothing that would take me away from my ministry, my family and my extended family. Nothing!

A few weeks later he calls me again, detailing that the job in Scranton is to replace a Music Minister and a Youth Minister and that the position is to help direct the retreats for every Catholic High School student in that diocese. He asks me if I would meet the priest and the nun involved in Scranton who were to visit the area the in ten days. I again politely say I will think about it, but in my heart, I am dead set against deciding for such a move.

A few days later I attend a parish picnic at Eisenhower Park in East Meadow hosted by St. Christopher's, Larry's parish. It was great. Spent my time that sunny day doing two things I love, playing guitar and playing softball.

Later that afternoon I am introduced to Elaine, a recent graduate of Penn State, who grew up in Franklin Square, Long Island. She is an impressive gal, kind of lit up like a Christmas tree in terms of her spirit. There is a special presence about her that just exudes peace and confidence. We begin to talk as we sit at a table, the sun descending behind the shade of the same tall trees that I first experienced as a child during end of year school picnics in this very park.

We share about our different ministries. She had been active in the Neumann Club on campus and as she is now home on Long Island, looking to meet other young people who share her beliefs. I tell her about Morningstar and also about the recent position I have been offered that I have no intent to pursue.

And so Elaine, my brand new friend, calmly and frankly smiles at me. She looks squarely into my eyes and whispers, "You know what you are supposed to do, don't you?" I pause… and sheepishly answer…"yes."

She then grasps for my hands, and I succumb; we both close our eyes and pray.

I speak aloud, "Lord…if you want me to go to Scranton, please let me know. If I am convinced it is Your Will, I will go." Elaine says not a word.

That was it, simple and direct. I trust that whatever God's Will was, that I will be able to discern it.

The very next morning, the director calls me again and so I finally agree to at least meet with Father Peter and Sister Andre. I reason that it is time to find out a little more about the programs they are offering for me to become a part of. The next week I meet them both.

I can say there was nothing in my spirit that made me want to jump up and say, "I'm your man." I was cordial and polite and I listened as they described the two programs they wanted me to coordinate. One was called *Journey* and the other called *Sunrise.*

*Journey* was the one-day retreat. I would be a part of a team that included two priests, two nuns and me. Every Catholic High School student would have to attend the event and most of the time it was in their home parish or school. We would travel throughout the diocese and cover all of the schools within their calendar year.

The other program, *Sunrise* was a weekend retreat. I would be responsible for reaching out to High School Seniors throughout the diocese to invite them to Our Lady of Fatima, the Scranton Retreat Center in Elmhurst, PA. I would take part in both giving talks and providing the music.

I thanked them for the information, was respectful and left as fast as I could for Long Island believing that I had done my duty to be open to the opportunity, but again…not gonna do it.

The next day, my friend Margaret called to invite me over with a few other friends to attend the first ever prayer meeting that she was going to have at her house. Margaret was very personable. She was in her early twenties, and beginning to grow in her faith for what she described as the first time. I agreed to bring my guitar and make a night of it.

There are only five of us that night, and after everyone arrives, we retreat to her den to begin the prayer meeting. As I sing the first song, I look over Margaret's shoulder at the poster on the wall. It's a poster of a *Sunrise*, and the only wording on it states, "Life is a *Journey*…Not a Destination."

I was sunk, didn't have a chance, despite my every desire to stay on Long Island. My God was calling me somewhere else, and I believed that to stay in His perfect Will, I would need to follow.

I do.

I believe in God...And I believe He sometimes calls us where we would rather not go. And you know the older we get the more we sometimes find this to be true.

## Chapter Twelve

# $40 a Week and Room & Board...

*When we make major decisions for the sake of God's will and not our own, God honors that. And then He provides for all that we need.*

Are new beginnings for you like breaths of fresh air?

Ok, so I was not going to be rich. Of course I wasn't looking for that, just a shot at an authentic position to use my gifts and to try and be a blessing to others. But... $40 a week? My monthly car payment itself was $140. That would give me $20 a month to live on. Yes, the room and board were covered; I wouldn't starve.

I don't really look for signs to lead me through life, but sometimes they come and you just have to go with them.

The year I spent at the Our Lady of Fatima Retreat Center was the most challenging year of my life up until that time. But it also held so many dramatic manifestations of God's loving providence that the small amount of money I made that year and the difficulties I encountered were just side bars to the great expression of the gift...of believing that I was learning to live in.

And those expressions started quickly. My end of summer orientation was a welcomed beginning. Without much work at all I was to take part in such a nice experience.

They called it "Family Vacations." The setting at Our Lady of Fatima was beautiful. The large brick-faced complex was nestled in the Poconos, and the grounds were spacious and treed with loads of room to relax and recreate. The smells of the mountain, summer air of Lackawanna County overwhelm in the best of ways. It seemed the perfect environment to experience God's gift of, and presence in nature.

For a very nominal fee, families in the diocese were invited for a week to experience each other in an environment that included prayer, games, sports and food. My first job was just to help facilitate some family activities and play touch football with the teens. Nice week, no stress, a lot of fun and a relaxed way to begin my new ministry.

A week after its conclusion, we are down to the work at hand. It is early September and the best way to start is with a staff retreat.

There I sit in a nicely furnished sitting room, with two priests, two nuns and a few other Youth Ministers for a one-day gathering of prayer and reflection. I feel for sure that I am in the right place.

We begin the retreat. It is directed and somewhat formal, but fun as well. And on the first page of the workbook there is a statement and an exercise. The statement is a spiritual truth.

"The Kingdom of God is here...but not yet."

It asks us to be descriptive to explain this truth in our own words, asking us to compare and contrast it with everyday life.

I close my eyes, rest and pray for a few moments. Then I write in my workbook:

> *The Kingdom of God is like a baby in its mother's womb. It is perfectly formed, ten little fingers, ten toes and absolutely beautiful. It is in the amniotic sac being nurtured by amniotic fluid. It is being sustained and protected by its mother until the time comes for its birth, until its life outside the womb begins...*

We are then asked to share our reflections. Mine is, I think, third or fourth and I share eagerly because I am not used to such profound thoughts and I'm happy that my introduction to my new team might be met with approval.

I am listened to intently and respectfully as we all are for each other.

When we all have had our turn to share, we are then asked to turn the page. The exercise continues, offering its own answer to the first question:

> *The Kingdom of God is like a baby in its mother's womb. It is in the amniotic sac, nurtured by the amniotic fluid....*

I feel like a fool. I sense that my new friends must think I read ahead, but I had not. I verbally note to them that I had not read ahead. I hope they believed me, but wasn't quite so sure.

No one said a word to my declaration of innocence.

Nonetheless my new ministry had begun for me on a holy, yet slightly uncertain note, but we were off and running.

I believe in God…and I believe in new beginnings.

# Chapter Thirteen

# The Mug...

*We've heard this many times... but God has a sense of humor.*

Where is your comfort zone?

I very quickly assimilated with my team. Although I was significantly younger than the other directors, it also included some Youth Ministers of my approximate age. I absolutely loved being with them and being a part of this new ministry.

I was though, often looked at with a skeptical eye. Some truly appreciated my New York roots and accent; others held more traditional distrust of those from my part of the country, and certainly with good reason. New Yorkers are not any less holy or more profane than other Americans, it is just that our pace is much more rapid and we need to cut to the chase more than most, just for survival sake.

And I was a different bird altogether. I was a New Yorker, but one who frankly believed in miracles. I felt a force within me to share and build faith with everyone around me. The urgency of my young, evangelistic spirit was I'm sure though… tinged with a New York state of mind.

I made friends very easily and just a few, seeming enemies just as fast. The overall spirit of the people I met was surely good and wholesome as so many people of the Poconos are by and large. I think mine was as well, yet I sometimes felt that I stood out like my own version of a sore thumb.

The retreats with the teens were going very well. It was such a joy to be able to share my own version of the Gospel, on a weekly basis with so many young people. There were literally hundreds of teenagers at the one-day retreats, and my role in the ministry was to share part of my conversion experience and then to provide music for the Sacraments of Reconciliation and the Eucharist at the end of the day.

It was as fulfilling as anything I had ever done in my life up until then. I was so caught up in both the joy of sharing my faith, and the wholesomeness of so many of the people I would meet, both young and old alike. Yet somehow I felt that my gifts might be better served with those less fortunate spiritually. I often wondered, "Do they really need me here?"

As the first few months were filled with seemingly perpetual joy, it almost felt uneasy. It was not something that I had been accustomed to. Almost everywhere I went people were polite, kind and easy to talk with. Not just those folks who I encountered as a Youth

Minister, but just plain people in public that I would meet day to day. It was just not what I had anticipated, not merely 120 miles outside of New York City.

Our Lady of Fatima was a huge building. As a former orphanage it could sleep a few hundred. There were a number of wings housing chapels, dorms, offices and long hallways. It would have cost a fortune to heat every part of the building during the winter. As our staff was small that would have been out to the question, especially during the periods of time that there were no weekend retreats going on, so resources needed to be conserved.

And so, as I would sit for hours during penance services for teens, strumming my guitar and singing from the St. Louis Jesuits Songs of Praise, I was often physically cold. Yes my heart was warm, and I yearned to share the tender sentiments of my soul to help prepare these young for this beautiful sacrament, but my fingers were often cold to the touch and I did my best to blow on them between hymns.

So one colder than usual night, I resolve to splurge… and dig into my monthly $20 surplus to purchase as large a mug as I could find to help me through the lengthy services.

On Saturday morning I ask one of my newfound friends to accompany me on my shopping "spree." Kate readily agrees and we find ourselves in a spacious general store in the heart of Scranton that early afternoon.

I find exactly what I am looking for, an over-sized gray and blue ceramic mug that will be just right. Off we go to the checkout counter and are second on line.

As we approach the woman clerk, being thrilled with my meager purchase, I smile at her and begin to make small talk. She stops me cold in my tracks with a rude answer. I smile and try again and she is even more discourteous as I recognized the happenstance of being thoroughly put in my place.

At my pause, the strangest feeling comes over me. A wave of peace envelops me as I am struck with as distinct an emotion as could be felt..."Ahhh... I am home."

It had been months since anyone had been rude to me. On Long Island that's a daily occurrence that you just learn to go with. Here, in downtown Scranton it is a surprising and welcomed revelation.

I chuckle as Kate and I leave with my mug, now feeling even more at home in my new surroundings.

During our next Penance service, I am warmed as much by the memory of it, as by my very large, hot cup of tea.

I believe in God...and I believe He can work through human nature.

## Chapter Fourteen

# Emboldened Belief...

*If you take care to follow the Lord on that narrow and focused road, you will grow to know when to really step out in faith.*

Has the connection and meaning of something ever unfolded for you, long after you first experienced it? Was there a reason for that?

It was February, 1981 and I had been in Scranton for six months. Our small team had traversed the diocese and by that point we had met with thousands of teenagers, bringing God's message of love and understanding. We were received very well at every turn as our program was well suited for this age group and our hearts, I believe were surely in the right place to share our core sentiments.

In sharing my faith during these retreats, I would often tell some of the stories of healing that I had experienced first hand. Although one of our sacraments, *The Anointing of the Sick* is just all about that, of how God heals those who come to Him, spiritually, emotionally, mentally and even physically, some people have a hard time wrapping their minds around that. The debate of medical science and faith has long been argued.

And so my sharings were received both well and with reservation. One of my team members, Sister Andre had such a great way with the teens. She could sit with a small group of boys and girls and elicit deep feelings to help them understand themselves. Sometimes she brought them to tears, and then just as quickly had them laughing at themselves and their own situations. We know everyone has their own special gifts and Andre was so gifted.

But up until that point in time she had really no direct experience in the types of extraordinary healings I would so freely talk about. To her credit, we worked very well together, but let's just say the jury was still out for her on this unusual New York Youth Minister and his unconventional stories.

I was looking forward to a very relaxed weekend, as we had no retreats scheduled for a few days. My expectation was to take it easy on this Friday night, and the only thing I had going the next few days was to play and sing at an Ultreya of the Cursillo movement on Saturday evening.

The Ultreya was so called as it signified the sharing of and living out of our Christian Faith. After one made a Cursillo retreat, he or she would participate in one or more of these follow up liturgies.

As often is the case, my plans were not God's plans. Andre calls up to my room just after dinner and asks me to come right down to the office, that we have some unexpected guests.

I hurry down and she explains that on the road right outside of our center, a bus just broke down. It's filled with a Youth Group and chaperones from a Bible believing church from Oklahoma. They had been en route to Scranton for a Christian convention. It would take until at least Monday to fix the bus and we are taking the kids in. She has other plans and asks if I could get them settled and then monitor them for the evening.

Of course I recognize the providence in the location of the break-down of their bus and agree. It's what I do. It would be a particular joy to be a part of helping them out.

Once they settle in, I gather them into one of the meeting rooms and we just hang out and get to know each other.

I had learned by that point in time, to listen to my intuition and I was not want to hold back any thoughts that might come to mind. And a very distinct thought did come to me, one I hadn't thought of for quite some time. It was the story of John's little nephew and the healing of his spinal meningitis.

And so I relay the story to them. And upon its conclusion the eight of them have really no discernable reaction. I am kind of surprised. Usually at one of my story's end there is some type of response, usually pretty positive, but they all just look at me kind of unaffected. I ask them why.

The tallest boy in the room, very well spoken for his sixteen years, answers me. He quickly says, "That's not a big deal with us. God answers prayer like that in our church every day."

I say, "Cool," and then just wonder if my discernment is off on this night. I feel for sure I am meant to share this story with them, it having come strongly to my mind and heart for the first time in two years. I resolve though, I must have just been wrong.

The bus is actually repaired rather quickly and by Saturday afternoon they are on their way. I am glad to have been a part of being in the right place at the right time for them but am still slightly baffled by my sharing of John's nephew's story.

After I say goodbye to them, I retreat to my room to read that day's readings and prepare the music for the evening Ultreya.

These Masses are very special as folks who have recently been through a Cursillo retreat are often deeply moved, many of them having had conversion experiences of some degree or another. Some are feeling God's love for the very first time in new and unexpected ways.

I know the atmosphere would be anticipatory and holy. I choose just the right hymns.

We gather this night, maybe fifteen of us in a sitting room of the rectory of the Cathedral in Scranton. The furniture is antique and plush with tapestry rugs and the atmosphere is warm.

Mass begins. We sing the opening hymn and enter into a beautiful hour of prayer and praise.

And then I am struck, dead in my tracks, with a woman's petition. Sometimes, during the *Prayer of the Faithful*, the priest will provide an opening for special intentions. A woman of about sixty-five years of age appeals to the small gathering.

"I would like everyone here to please pray for my granddaughter. She has spinal meningitis," she pleads, her voice quivering, barely getting her words out.

I blink. I know I am about to embark upon totally new territory for me. I have no doubt of what I will do right after Mass.

Upon its conclusion, I put down my guitar and quietly walk over to this woman sitting on the overstuffed, Victorian chair. I approach her slowly and then kneel at her feet.

I introduce myself to her saying, "Hi, I'm Rob McGuffey from Our Lady of Fatima and I have very good news for you." She smiles and looks questioningly into my eyes.

I proceed to tell her about my experience from the night before with the Oklahoma teenagers, and how I had told them about John's little nephew and his healing of the same illness two years prior.

And then I offer, "I believe that if you pray with me right now, God is going to heal your granddaughter."

I had never, ever been so bold in my life. I had prayed for thousands of things in the five years since my own conversion, but never was so daring to speak for my God in such an audacious manner. But it was such that I just couldn't help myself. And unburdening this prayer from my heart through my lips brought immediate peace to me, if not surprise and a degree of puzzlement to her. Although saying, thank you, she seemed to be a bit bewildered by the encounter. And frankly, so was I.

As winter began to fade and spring arrived, those months continued to be filled with spiritually profitable experiences tinged with the suffering that I was learning would accompany ministries of this kind. I did experience great peace and new heights in my personal prayer, yet also experienced some subtle discrimination from some folks that didn't necessarily share my obviously progressive views on prayer and healing. I did on occasion go to sleep that year, with tears in my eyes, for both those who accepted the radical message of Christ and His Love, and those who rejected it.

And so, in early April I find myself in our spacious kitchen. It is just an ordinary Saturday morning, but one of the first few warm days of spring. In fact the back door to the kitchen is wide opened, with only the screen door closed.

Unannounced, a woman swings open the door and enters as it clacks in behind her. She is maybe fifteen yards from me when she comes in. She takes a few steps, looks up and locks eyes with mine. And then she runs towards me shrieking, "It's you; it's you!!!" I am a bit stunned as I don't recognize her at all, as she continues hurriedly in my direction.

When she reaches me she wraps her arms around me and hugs and squeezes me as a grandmother would her favorite grandson after a long absence. And I am still a bit taken aback. I have to let her know that I don't know who she is. Without concern she reminds me. "I am the woman you prayed with at the Cathedral rectory over the winter when you said my granddaughter would be healed of Spinal Meningitis. The day after you prayed, my granddaughter was completely healed."

I quickly remind her that it was her petition and that we both had prayed together, that it wasn't me, but I believed it to a special grace of God. It is such a joy to share in her elation and I recall in that moment, my critical reluctance to even consider moving to Scranton when first presented with the opportunity.

After the woman thanks me again and goes on her way, I am left in the kitchen alone with Andre.

Up until that point, to my knowledge Sr. Andre hadn't experienced any real evidence of spontaneous physical healing in her life or in her circle of influence. I need to explain the situation to her, telling her of the story of the woman's prayer of petition as I remind Andre of the teens from Oklahoma. I then tell her of how John's nephew was healed of the same illness years before.

Before my eyes, tears well up in hers and she seems to just get it… and to believe.

I believe in God…and I believe that things happen when they are supposed to, not when I would like them to.

## Chapter Fifteen

# All Good Things...

*The full expression of your gifts brings a sense of harmony that can yield the gift of discernment.*

Is there something, or Someone within beyond your present comprehension?

I sensed that my time in Scranton was coming to a close. I truly wasn't homesick, had gotten back to Carle Place maybe once a month on the benevolence of more than one secret Santa, and because of that was able on a number of occasions to sing with Larry in a few coffee houses. But after the school year, I felt I had done what I was called to do there.

I certainly prayed about it, as I had begun to learn not to lean unto my own understanding, but I was satisfied with the answer to my prayers.[4]

4. Proverbs 3:5

I had been journaling in an attempt to discern God's will about returning home. I would write about my experiences and about the pull I felt to move back to Long Island. And a curious thing happened. At first I thought it was my pride as I began to count the people on Long Island that might benefit from my moving back. I wrote perhaps twenty names and what it might mean to each of us if I returned. And I knew them all…except for one.

The last thing I wrote in this journal entry was, *"Billy needs me… whoever the heck Billy is."*

I would find out several months after I did make the decision to return to Long Island. Billy was a young man who became engaged to my friend Nora. I would later marry Nora's sister, Paula. And Billy became my brother-in-law. And yes, on a number of occasions, Billy needed me, maybe more than most.

I believe in God…and I believe that sometimes he gives us little clues…just to show us that He is there.

# Chapter Sixteen

# Right Place, Right Time...

*Higher are His ways above our ways...*
*as high as the heavens are above the earth.*[5]

Whose time is it anyway?

In my limited experience over the last thirty-nine years of learning to exercise and develop the gift...of believing, I've had many prayers answered in the affirmative, many in the negative and so many that I believe have been answered...not yet. Isn't that where faith comes in? Isn't that the environment where we begin to discover and strengthen our spiritual muscles? And isn't that itself...a gift?

One area that I've had to grow in faith in is the area of trust that those close to me would have just a taste of the gift...of believing, that I have been gifted with. It became a passion of mine from the

5. Paraphrase of Isaiah 55:9

moment of my conversion, and so many of my family, close friends and relatives have themselves experienced their own awakening of God's Love in their lives. Some have even been touched by my life and sometimes by my stories.

And then, some in my family precipitated my awakening of faith and I'm sure that their prayers were instrumental in my own conversion. One jolly old soul was Brother Polycarp.

Polycarp, born Bill Miller was my great uncle and Godfather to my Mom. He was an Alexian Brother, a physical therapist who had dedicated his life to God and to serving in the medical profession. His hearty laugh and big spirit was such that everyone knew when he was in the room.

I was to find out something, just days after my conversion how it took over thirty years for Polycarp to find God.

He had made his decision to dedicate his life to God soon after his final tour of duty at the end of WWII where he served in Italy. He had a yearning for the priesthood but feared he wouldn't have the aptitude for the great amount of study required. So before returning to the US, he sought out the saintly and now Saint Padre Pio for prayer and advice. And Padre Pio did pray with him, and wrote to him to trust in the Lord who would surely help him with his studies.

In ultimately becoming a religious brother, Polycarp heard and answered a calling of a slightly different sort helping so many for so long. His calling and concentration became the healing of the body through the growing field of physical therapy. He attained numerous degrees, while ministering and studying throughout

William C. Millar

If the Lord has called you
and given you the great grace
of a vocation, He will give
you the necessary strength
to overcome all obstacles
and difficulties even if
they seem unsuperable.
I will pray for you and
want you to join your
prayers to mine. When
your studies seem hard,
remember that you are not
alone...

Father Pio.

his long life, and was eventually appointed the Chaplain to the National Society of Physical Therapists.

Less than two weeks after my own conversion, I am so desirous to talk with someone who might understand the deep sense I now have of God. I ask my Mom if she knows anyone who might be able to relate to me. She promptly tells me that my Uncle Polycarp is coming to visit in a few days. I hadn't seen him in almost two years.

Polycarp walks in the front door with as wide a smile as I've seen on his face. He gives me a wink, and I sense that Mom must have prepped him about the change of heart I've begun to undergo.

It is not long after he is settled in for the few days he would spend with us that we find ourselves in the dining room for our first of what would become many fireside chats that would just warm my soul.

Polycarp was one of a kind, but he seemed to have a new sense about him, a much more peaceful sense and thus he was much better able to be present with me than he had been before.

Novice that I am, I don't ask him how he is; I just eagerly begin to tell him of this new sense that I have, that God is real.

He listens intently and tells me he can relate. But what he says astonishes me. He states that from the day he took his vows, thirty years prior, he went to Mass every single day…and did not know God until just a few months ago.

And so I ask, "What are you saying?" And it seems the love just pours out of him as he recounts how in a solitary moment, the

Spirit of God touched him. He shares, "It was seemingly out of nowhere, yet when God touched me...I knew it was Him. It could be no other. The love was all encompassing and complete. I had never experienced anything like it, nor anyone like Him before..."

As he shared this with me, I was a bit dumbfounded. What could it mean? I was twenty-two at the time, having previously avoided the Church like the plague, yet I would begin to so quickly discover the realness of God. And my great uncle after so long and holy a life had just experienced something of the same just a short time ago? There was no logic in that; it made no sense to me.

Yet that was as it was. He was certainly no worse for wear. His joy abounded, he had found his life long friend and he could think of nothing else. He lived in the present, and he lived in God's presence throughout the rest of his life, ministering God's love in such new and exciting ways.

Less than a year after I was born, my younger brother James comes into the world. We are Irish twins, his birth, just eleven months after mine. Yet it is not without peril. He arrives three months prematurely in 1955 with a number of serious challenges including a collapsed lung and he was unable to breath on his own.

James William entered the world on Good Friday. His medical team did not give him much chance to survive. Our doctor suggested that my mother should not be unnerved any further after my brother's very difficult birth and so they kept the dire prognosis from her. That until a well meaning nurse spoke to my mother as the boy lay helpless in his incubator. She said, "Don't worry ma'am, sometimes babies like that live..."

My Mom is devastated, but begins a novena of prayers that my family believes to this day helped to save and heal my brother. On Easter Sunday James takes a turn for the better and begins his life free of serious illness.

All during our coffee house years, James was with us in our ministry. He seemed as devout a Christian as I knew. He then began his own ministries as a lay missionary in both Mexico and Canada. He much later felt the call to the priesthood and at forty years of age was ordained. And yet he confessed to me that the first time he actually "felt" God's presence was that day that he became a priest, almost twenty years after making his decision to follow God.

Again, how could this be? It really made no natural sense to me.

In the Gospel of John, Christ speaks to Nicodemus and also to us saying:

> *"You must be born from above. The wind blows where it wills, and you can hear the sound it makes, but you do not know where it comes from or where it goes; so it is with everyone who is born of the Spirit."*
>
> *Nicodemus answers and says to him, "How can this happen?"*
>
> *Jesus answers and says, "You are teacher of Israel and you do not understand this? Amen, amen I say to you, we speak of what we know and we testify to what we have seen, but you people do not accept our testimony. If I tell you about earthly things and you do not believe, how will you believe if I tell you about heavenly things? No one has gone up to heaven except the one who has come down*

> *from heaven, the Son of Man. And just as Moses lifted up the serpent in the desert, so must the Son of Man be lifted up, so that everyone who believes in him may have eternal life."*[6]

And so everyone has his own time, the right place, the right time. There are so many teachings on persistence in prayer, so whether the time is now or tomorrow we must persist in believing. We must persist in asking for the gift…of believing, of deeper believing that we can be in tune and in touch with God's Wisdom and His perfect timing for ourselves and those that we love.

I believe in God…and I yield to Him today for myself and for those I entrust into His hands.

6. John 3:7b-15

## Chapter Seventeen

# Forgive Them Father...

*A key element in believing... is forgiveness.*

*Toward the end of my writing of this first of what I hope will be a series of "Gift" books, I awoke one Saturday morning with these thoughts on my heart. I'm very thankful for them as they helped me to crystallize some views about forgiveness that I had not yet entertained.*

"Forgive them Father for they know not what they do."[7]

Or forgive them Father because they don't know what they are doing.

I believe that everything that Christ said was true. But this, one of the last things He said on the cross was so telling, about us and our condition of sometimes doing ill-advised things in order to fall and then grow in awareness, and so telling about Him as He

7. Luke 23:34

transcended His earthly condition by virtue of His divinity. Yet He embraced our condition enough to understand us completely, our lower selves and our ultimate potential to rise to new awareness… but we need His forgiveness to do so.

"Forgive them Father; they know not what they do."

Papa's wife, Mama, at eighty-six, used an expression frequently in her itinerate sharing of her faith. In her very thick German accent, with eyes raised, in resignation and some regret, but also in great reverence for its wisdom she would lament, "Too soon olt…too late schmaat," or less phonetically, too soon old, too late smart.

Haven't we all felt that at junctures in our lives? But it is never too late. Reflection on God's forgiveness at every turn in which it is required is the very fuel of our existence. His never ending supply of virtue is that "well" within us that springs up unto eternal life. And so what is eternal if not never ending source of life giving love?

The Big Lie is that we love in vain.

The Big Truth is that although it sometimes may be painful, when we love we reign, whether we feel it in that moment or not. Whether we experience great joy or are anguished in great pain, the decision to love anoints the expression for both the lover and the loved. The latter just may hurt more. Oh well...

When we believe... and persevere in acts of love we put ourselves in a place where all things are possible and so much more is made evident.

Don't leave your character behind. Don't let one thing or more that someone has done or said affect you in a way that you forget who you are and all of the wonderful lessons you've learned along your way.

If you don't bring your virtue with you it's like a prized possession left hiding in a cupboard. It is still prized, yet unable to express its beauty. And isn't your virtue, your character your most valuable asset? Nothing else comes close.

Is it not the reason you were born? Is it not the only thing you can take with you as you leave your home each day, or as you leave this world behind? The way you enter today is a foreshadowing expression of the way you will enter into the next life.

So one must believe...One must believe in the simple act of loving when it is oh so hard to do so.

You must believe that patience is called for when all of those around you have seemed to have turned aside from right thinking and right expression.

You must allow that inexhaustible supply of holy unction you have been blessed with to simmer to the surface of you soul and be freely given as...gift to those who have been entrusted to you.

"Forgive them Father, they know not what they do."

One of my favorite compositions is, I believe, my most fervent. I'd like to pray it for you.

## Father of Mercy

O Father of Mercy, Come in and make me whole
O Father of Mercy, Touch my very soul

O Father of Mercy, Enlighten us with Light
O Father of Mercy, Guide us through the night

In our lives, You teach us…the way that we should go
We learn therein to rest…and to wait upon Your Word

Your Word always searches…deep inside our hearts
Bringing truth and loving kindness
To show us who we are
We're children…of a loving Father

O Father of Mercy…You've touched and made us whole
O Father of Mercy…Embraced our very soul

O Father of Mercy…You've enlightened us with light
O Father of Mercy…With Your Love ere burning bright

In our lives, you've taught us…the way that we should go
We've learned therein to rest
And to wait upon Your Word

Your Word always searches…deep inside our hearts
Bringing truth and loving kindness…to show us who we are

We're children…of a Loving Father…Who shows us Mercy
Forever

I believe in God…and I do believe in His mercy.

## Chapter Eighteen

# Finding Your Place... Is Part of His Grand Plan

*Be open at every moment of your walk.*
*When you think you might be winding down,*
*you may just be beginning...*

The first story of this, my first Inspirational, started with an image, one whose import I did not immediately understand, although it did begin to unfold in real time rather quickly. And as I took and take the whole experience on faith, I still try to examine it for deeper meanings, deeper understandings, and a deeper relationship with the One who continues to call me on my way.

And so perhaps it's appropriate to end here with another image, one that I woke up to on the second of July in 2014, some thirty-six years after the fortuitous series of events that saved Roseann's life. The image doesn't necessarily concern Roseann, although she did call the other day, less than an hour after I said to myself, "I have to call her..."

No, this image was for me. And it came immediately after a direct and heartfelt prayer.

I had been feeling quite challenged lately, not only with personal trials, but with an earnest surveying of a culture that has, by and large, turned aside from ways that would help it to arrive at a more deeply fulfilled destiny. And so my prayer at 7am was a simple...

"Help...what should I do?"

And by the great grace of God, my answer came as if He anticipated my cry, which, yes...I believe He did.

This image is clear, and like the one for Roseann, it is as if I am watching a movie, this time though, in color. I had already been awake for an hour, thinking, plotting my day, praying for others and then, of course, for myself. A scene is set before me.

I am standing on a dock, overlooking an ocean, yet the dock is covered like some sort of hanger and opened to the vast waters. It is large, old, made of wood, with a steel foundation, with red rust and barnacles imbedded almost to its core. But it is steady and true to its purpose, as the waters splash underneath it and on its sides.

There are other people, invisible though they are, who had worked on this dock, and are now, in a sense, there with me. They had toiled long and hard and were true to themselves, their families and to their God.

And as I am standing on its crusty, damp surface, the dock becomes slightly loose from its moorings and begins to disengage. I can feel uneasiness as my footing becomes somewhat unstable. As I steady myself, turning to my right, there is a new structure, already laid at a right angle to the old dock, and the entire dock is moving toward it. My stance is relatively unmoved with just the turn of my gaze. It begins to now focus on the new structure, which appears to be some sort of rail along the shoreline. It stretches as far as the eye can see at least until the morning mist makes it seem to disappear.

As the old dock and I end our short shifting of just a few feet, I need just step onto this rail. ...Instead, I take a moment to survey what unfolds before me. I am at once, taken up in its power and beauty.

This rail is steel as well, but streamlined and glistening with newness. It is perfect, stable and strong, anchored in the sand earth, with a nature that exudes permanence. And when after just a few moments, I have a beginning sense of the meaning of this part of the image, the old dock begins to re-engage, traveling the foot or so back to its original spot. I don't want to go, but the unsettling feeling of movement under my feet gives way to the feeling of comfort of still standing on my same spot, and having stayed in place...my place.

And without going into great detail with my personal discernment of the meaning of this image, suffice it to say that I am also the old dock, and of course, He is the new and permanent rail. And I'm ok with going back to my place for now, and thankful that He is who He is.

I believe in God...and if He believes in me...then I do too.

*Thanks for listening to some of my early stories of my learning to believe. I am convinced that everything that happens to us is a gift, whether at the time seemingly good… or difficult to accept.*

*And I am so glad to be able to have shared*
*some of the gifts I've been given with you.*

*All the best,*
*Your friend,*

# Acknowledgements

I want to thank my wife Paula and my children Robbie, Bethie, Jenna, Kristi and Andrew...for your love and support and for always keeping me humble...anyone got any laundry?

Thanks Mom and Dad, Danny, James, Tina and Mary for being reflections of God's love for me...and without whom I would not have found my gifts.

Thank you sweet Roseanne...for following our Lord through thick and thin.

I want to thank all of my friends who previewed my first work, offering so much love and encouragement.

To all of my dear friends at the School of Missionary Disciples of the Diocese of Rockville Centre, formerly the Pastoral Formation Institute. It is an honor to study, to learn, to reflect and to pray with you. May Our Lord richly bless you with deeper gifts... of believing.

To the pastors who have shepherded me...I thank you.

To my brothers and sisters of Our Lady of Mercy parish who I have the privilege of walking and growing in faith with. Thank you.

I want to thank my new brother Rob, who came into my life at the perfect time and for his wisdom and guidance, his friendship and his loyalty...and his belief in the One who guides us all.

And I want to thank you. I pray God's most choice blessings on you, your families and your friends. I pray...and believe that your life will be surrounded by His never ending love and support as you discover the gifts you have been given, always finding yourself and your God in the process.

# Endnotes

1. Ecclesiastes 3:1
2. Matthew 5:3
3. Psalm 91:16
4. Proverbs 3:5
5. Paraphrase of Isaiah 55:9
6. John 3:7b-15
7. Luke 23:34

# The Gift... of Believing
## Endorsements

*"As I read Rob McGuffey's book I was reminded of a section in the book* New Seeds of Contemplation *by Thomas Merton. He writes that God is always showering us with graces like many seeds that flow from heaven and so many of them that we do not take hold of. Rob's book reminded me of the many ways that God comes to our lives, the simple ways he comes to us every day. These are constant signs of God's love. Reading Rob's book will inspire many to see God in the many events that take place in our lives daily. It is a very worthwhile read and I recommended it highly."*

**Reverend Robert Blyman**
Faculty, North American College, Rome, Italy

*"I first met Rob McGuffey on my senior-year retreat in 1980. What a joy to meet him again in these pages. They brought back many memories. Rob has an eye for the invisible workings of providence. He'll have you entertained and astonished"*

**Mike Aquilina**
Author, *Angels of God*, and EWTN Host

"The Gift...of Believing *is a powerful little book about how God works in us every day. Rob has taken the mysterious relationship that we call faith and its component that is called prayer and has shown us how God is present and how he touches us in everyday and unexpected ways, and how prayer is simply learning to be open to his touch and aware of his presence. It's what we call 'grace' and this is a book filled with moments of grace, memories of grace, surprises of grace and the peace that comes from letting His grace into our hearts. Read this book and be prepared to have your own surprises of grace!"*

**Monsignor Thomas C. Costa**
Vicar for Senior Priests, Rockville Centre Diocese NY

*"In a simple and honest way, Rob shares his testimony of faith. I enjoyed every story so much. In* The Gift... of Believing *we witness the power of faithful prayer."*

**Diana Pizarro**

Associate Director of Faith Formation, Diocese of Rockville Centre, NY

"The Gift... of Believing *is an authentic and personal narrative filled with hope and more than a few honest-to-goodness miracles. When I read it for the first time, my spiritual tank overflowed with warmth that can only be described as blessed. When I was finished, my heart clamored for more 'Believing' so I read it again and again. Each time you read* The Gift...of Believing, *it will offer you spiritual food for your soul and inspiration that will change your life forever..."*

**Rob Palasciano**

Inspirational Speaker and Author of *From Anger To Enlightenment*

*"... These words of Pope Francis are a perfect description of Rob's book,* The Gift... of Believing *and of his journey...*

> *'Those who believe, see; they see with a light that illumines their entire journey for it comes from the risen Christ, the Morning Star which never sets.' Pope Francis*

*"Rob writes with the passion of his faith. He wants to share what he has been given and instills a sense of 'giftedness' in the reader. He describes so vividly that I found myself entering each scene. This book has reinforced my own gratitude for the gift of Life and the gift of Faith."*

**Sr. Jeanne A. Brendel O.P.**

Executive Director Harvest Houses, Syosset, NY

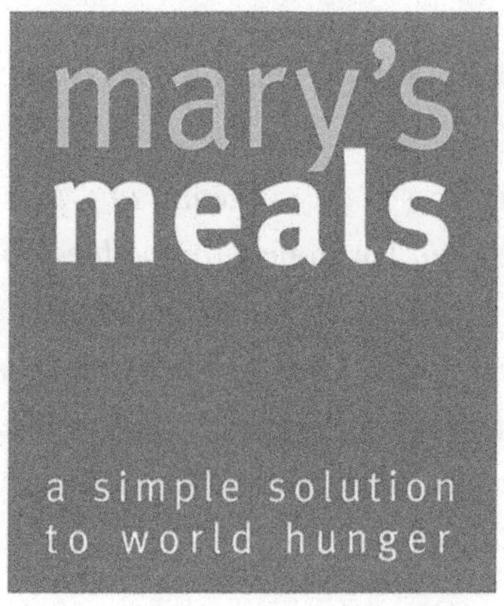


A portion of the proceeds from *The Gift... of Believing* supports Mary's Meals, the international charity which provides a daily meal in school to more than one million impoverished children around the world. Please visit www.marysmeals.org to find out more.

https://robmcguffey.org

Made in the USA
Las Vegas, NV
12 February 2022